Doorways
Through Time

DOORWAYS
THROUGH TIME
The Romance of Archaeology

Stephen Bertman

JEREMY P. TARCHER, INC.
Los Angeles

The author would like to thank the following for their gracious permission to reprint:

Harcourt Brace Jovanovich and Faber and Faber, Ltd., for lines quoted from "Little Gidding" in *Four Quartets* by T. S. Eliot, copyright 1943 by T. S. Eliot, renewed 1971 by Esme Valerie Eliot.

New Directions Publishing Corporation for an extract from Ezra Pound and Noel Stock, *trans., Love Poems of Ancient Egypt,* copyright © 1962 by Ezra Pound and Noel Stock;

Chappell & Co., Inc., for a selection from the lyrics of *Camelot* by Alan Jay Lerner & Frederick Lowe, copyright © 1960 & 1961 by Alan Jay Lerner & Frederick Lowe; Chappell & Co., Inc., owner of publication and allied rights throughout the world; International Copyright Secured. ALL RIGHTS RESERVED. Used by permission.

Library of Congress Cataloging in Publication Data

Bertman, Stephen.
   Doorways through time.
   Bibliography: p.
   Includes index.
   1. Archaeology. I. Title.
CC165.B47   1987   930.1   86–23000
ISBN 0–87477–622–8

Jeremy P. Tarcher, Inc.
5858 Wilshire Blvd., Suite 200
Los Angeles, CA 90036

Design by Thom Dower

Manufactured in the United States of America
10 9 8 7 6 5 4 3 2

For Elaine, Laura, and Matt

We shall not cease from exploration
And the end of all our exploring
Will be to arrive where we started
And know the place for the first time.

T. S. Eliot, Four Quartets

Table of Contents

Illustrations

Cover photo: View of the ruins of Palenque by Frederick Catherwood (from his *Views of Ancient Monuments in Central America, Chiapas, and Yucatan,* 1844).

Acknowledgments

ARCHAEOLOGY AFFIRMS our debt to the past, and those who write about archaeology are indebted too—to those who went before and showed them the way. A boyhood book, *Lost Worlds* by Anne Terry White, an antique copy of *The Book of Knowledge,* and a compassionate Latin teacher, Miss Helen Robbie, helped me first to learn about the ancient world. At New York and Columbia universities I was lucky to know teachers who believed in popularizing the Classics—Jotham Johnson, Casper J. Kraemer, Jr., Lionel Casson, Gilbert Highet, and Moses Hadas—and one who helped teach me the discipline of writing, Macha L. Rosenthal. To Cyrus H. Gordon I owe a great debt: at Brandeis University he helped me to see beyond artificial academic boundaries to discover wider truths and has since continued to give me encouragement.

To my parents I am grateful for the financial and personal sacrifices that made my education possible; to my wife, Elaine, for loving support through difficult times.

Lastly I wish to thank my secretary, Ana Besné, who typed with affection most of the original manuscript of this book, and whose experiences as a girl on the coast of Spain inspired my first chapter. Sudden death prevented her from holding the printed copy in her hand.

Like Ana, some of the people named here will not be able to read my thanks, but this book is theirs nonetheless.

Foreword

MANY POPULAR BOOKS have been written on the romance of archaeology, but Stephen Bertman's is not only better but different. Many who write about archaeological discoveries on every continent, from prehistoric times to the full light of recorded history, are amateurs untrained in any aspect of the subject. The opposite extreme is the professional archaeologist who knows one area well and little about anything else.

No one can master all the cultures of the Near East, India, the Far East, Europe, Africa, and the Americas. But it is possible for the gifted scholar to master an extensive and important segment of world archaeology and to go on from there to the rest of the world, applying the high standards of his specialty.

Dr. Bertman is a trained scholar in the three main divisions of our own Western civilization: Israel, Greece, and Rome. He not only knows Hebrew, Greek, and Latin but has absorbed the values inherent in all three literatures. His knowledge has not made of him a limited specialist but rather has opened the doors to a curiosity in and understanding of all humanity.

Stephen Bertman has many unusual qualities. He is responsible in regard to factual details and at the same time a lucid writer, whose scholarship has not stifled the poet within him. It is the combination of savant, poet, and generalist that makes Bertman unique and *Doorways through Time* enlightening and enjoyable to read.

No one will complain that this book does not contain enough material. On the contrary, it is a very rich feast. Bertman's taste and judgment in selecting his subtopics are superb.

In congratulating Stephen Bertman for writing this fascinating book, I also felicitate the reader on the pleasure of savoring it.

Cyrus H. Gordon
Professor of Hebraic Studies and
Director of the Center for Ebla Research
New York University

The Fragile Past

AS I SIT before my typewriter, the tokens of my life lie scattered on the desk before me: coins and keys, wallet and pen—for better or worse, the pocket symbols of who I am. What could someone learn, I wonder, from these material things I call my own? What could they learn of me?

Could they learn from the keys the amiable locks I turn each day to find my way through life? Could they tell the thoughts that flow from my pen? Could they measure the love I feel for faces pressed tight between wallet calendars and cards?

I think of my children and wonder who they will become. They never knew my father (as I never knew his), and their memories of a second grandfather are few. Great-grandparents are to them only branches on a construction-paper tree glued together once upon a time in school.

How tenuous is our knowledge of our own human past. And how impoverished we are for our ignorance.

The ancient Greeks keenly understood life's transience. Their poet Homer put it into words. "Even as are the generations of leaves," he said, "such are those likewise of men; the leaves that be the wind scattereth on the earth, and the forest buddeth and putteth forth more again, when the season of spring is at hand; so of the generations of men one putteth forth and another ceaseth."[1]

In the autumn wind of time it is the human spirit that first departs. How ironic that what is most precious to us should also be the least permanent part of our being. Radiant, evanescent, the spirit vanishes, leaving behind at death its vehicle, the body, which in turn more slowly decays.

It is *in*organic matter that endures, the substance farthest removed from the soul. Sensing this, some have sought to defy their dissolution by building tombs. Others over the ages have sought to leave a part of their soul behind, impressing into matter their feelings and thoughts. Thus the arts represent the subconscious or deliberate quest for immortality. Contemplating his poems the Roman poet Horace said, "Not wholly do I die."[2] Yet nature itself works against this wish: Manuscripts crumble, sculptures corrode, even inscriptions cut in stone wear away.

In nature, time is the great leveler. How difficult then to reconstruct the substance of a life from remaining objects that themselves decay. And how much more difficult to recover the form of lives lived long ago. For if whole civilizations that endured by the cumulative weight of their creations lie in ruins, where may the imprint of individual lives be traced?

Curiously, it is the past itself that obscures its discovery, for it comes to us in unwilling disguise. Scripts once easily read become unintelligible ciphers and living languages forgotten tongues. In time, even ancient statues, bleached of vital colors by millennia of sun and rain, look bloodless and inhuman. Seemingly without feeling, they stand bereft of heads and arms. Yet precisely because of this mutilation they beckon us on. Perfect and intact, the Winged Victory of Samothrace might be only a remarkable work of art; but broken, her wings upswept, her gown windblown against her torso, she appears to resist annihilation itself with a fierce and sensuous fury. "Look," she cries out to us, "I have survived time itself. *This* is my truest victory."

Indeed, even our words become obstacles as we seek to recapture time, for in the very act of calling a thing ancient we change it from what it was.

In reality the past is "ancient" only because we stand where we do as we look back at it. To those who once lived it, the past was the present, alive and new. In just the same way, *we* will be called ancient some day, sterilized in a textbook and neatly summed up, despite the fact that we share fragile lives with those we love, not seeing beyond tomorrow.

The present is in flux. The past, however, can be seen in historical perspective, complete with beginning, middle, and end, its causes and consequences ready for dissection. Because of this the past is more intelligible than the present, but—for all that—less immediate, less alive. Yet the past *was* the present once. We can see that if only we restore to the past its proper dimension, returning to it its spontaneity and its life.

We must train ourselves to see our faces in an earlier day. Standing in a winter wind, we must draw our strength from dead and swirling leaves that once grew green, for it is from them alone that the fullness of another spring can come.

In Search of Time

ARCHAEOLOGY IS ROOTED in humanity's curiosity about its origins. "Were things always this way?" "Are there remains of an earlier time?" "Who lived here before?" "Are the stories of the past really true?"—these questions and more were the seeds from which grew archaeological science. The same curiosity that led you to pick up this book, to turn and read these pages, motivated those who went before and made the discoveries from which this book was written.

The methods an archaeologist uses are mostly common sense refined by experience. In fact, the single most important method of archaeology can be understood by looking into so mundane an object as a wastepaper basket. Carefully inspect its contents and you can deduce what has happened in recent days. At the top, perhaps, is the crumpled receipt from a shopping trip. Beneath it lie the unwanted advertisements from the afternoon mail. Below may be the wrappers from some candy consumed last night. At the very bottom, the draft of a letter written yesterday.

Taken in reverse order, from bottom to top, these remains of everyday life portray a sequence of events. First a letter was composed; then candy was consumed; later, mail was

Excavations at Troy in the days of Schliemann.

read; and finally, shopping was done. Similar deductions could be made by examining the layers of your kitchen garbage, though the exercise would be far less appealing.

In removing the wastepaper basket's contents, noting their relative position, and interpreting their significance, you have in fact practiced a bit of domestic archaeology, different only in scope from the kind practiced by archaeologists in the field. Archaeologists call the layers of debris *strata* (singular, *stratum*) and their careful removal *stratigraphic excavation*. The system of dating we followed—calling what is lower older and what is higher newer—is known as *relative chronology*.

If, however, we wanted to know how much time—minutes, hours, or days—actually elapsed between one deposit and another, we would need more information. To the archaeologist the dating of deposits by years, centuries, or millennia is known as *absolute chronology* and is crucial to the reconstruction of history.

In dating layers of time, the archaeologist is helped by the discovery of inscriptions that refer to persons or events familiar to historians. Such inscriptions may be found on buried monuments or coins. Sometimes other physical evidence (such as the destruction of a city) can point to a datable event in history. Once a layer has been dated (say, to the fifth century B.C.), the layers above and below can be dated by extrapolation (before the fifth century for what is lower; after the fifth century for what is higher).

By now you may be wondering why cities would have layers, but here too the answer is easy to understand. In places that have been occupied over long periods of time, the level on which successive generations live actually rises as streets are repaved and new buildings are built over the remains of earlier ones. Perhaps in the center of *your* city or town there are layers of time hidden beneath sidewalks and streets.

This was especially true in ancient communities where building materials were often fragile and fires frequent. Rather than remove debris, new or returning settlers would level the ground and build above it. In the absence of garbage collection, ancient streets and even house floors were often covered over with new clay to hide unsightly litter; when the street outside your door got too high, it was time to build again.

As time passed, the style of artifacts, such as pottery, would change. As such artifacts were lost or broken and thrown away, their remnants became mixed with the debris of streets and refuse heaps.

The archaeologist who digs through strata can actually see the stylistic evolution of certain artifacts through time. Certain styles of pottery, for example, denote particular periods during which they were made and used. When such a telltale style is uncovered, the archaeologist has a means of dating the context in which it was found.

The work of the archaeologist is in many ways like that of a detective. Before he can reconstruct the "crime," he must discover the evidence and carefully record what he has found. Even the smallest bit of evidence must be properly noted and cataloged, for what may seem unimportant today may become vitally important tomorrow in reconstructing the past.

The archaeologist's excavation tools will not be the crude shovel or spade but the trowel, the whiskbroom, and even the brush. The exact location of every find must be diligently recorded, for once a site is excavated it ceases to exist. Only if it can be visually resurrected from the archaeologist's final report will it live once again. Although the writing and editing of a report back home in an office may not be as exciting as excavation in the field, without it all the digging will be in vain, because without publication no one will ever know what once existed.

Patience and persistence are among the most essential qualities of the professional archaeologist; to these add intellect and intuition. Yet the excavator will not be alone in performing the task. The excavator's team may include a surveyor and a photographer, an artist and an epigrapher, and specialists in such fields as ceramics and conservation.

Skill in management and talent for diplomacy will also be needed attributes.

*   *   *   *

As a science, archaeology began largely in the nineteenth century, driven by an interest in our human history and the history of nations at a time when the natural sciences were flourishing. The landscape of that century and of the early twentieth century are marked by the footprints of giants whose like we shall not see again: Schliemann and Stephens, Petrie and Carter, Woolley and Evans, self-made men largely of independent wealth who thrived in an era of individualism. Each could not rest in his own time, drawn on instead by the lure of the past. The discoveries of these men were to be enhanced by the decipherment of ancient scripts, giving scholars further access to the mind of the ancient world.

But just as discoveries have continued to be made in this century, so have the methods of archaeology continued to grow. In the beginning, Classical guidebooks, surviving place-names, and visible ruins led to the discovery of lost cities and civilizations. Today, ruins hidden to the eye can be detected from the air by radar, sensitized photography, and sophisticated satellite reconnaisance; in the sea by scuba divers, submersibles, and sonar; and on land by electronic instruments that scan the depths of the earth for evidence of man-made works. Dating techniques too have been improved through the development of new types of laboratory analysis that measure time from the residual radioactivity in organic samples or the electron activity in ancient pottery. Some laboratory tests permit us now to separate true ancient masterpieces from modern fakes by identifying the processes and materials used in manufacture. With the aid of mathematical theory and modeling, attempts are even being made to discover and describe patterns in the past to explain not only the "what" but the "why" of cultural change. Mathematics and the natural sciences have all been enlisted in the search for lost worlds.

Yet it is easy for modern archaeologists, surrounded by so many quantitative techniques, to be dazzled into forgetting their qualitative mission. Their purpose is and always should be fundamentally a human one: to discover and narrate with honesty and compassion the story of lives once lived. The archaeologist's duty is to keep faith with the ghosts, to serve as a medium for those who no longer have voices of their own.

That is *my* purpose too: to help you feel the tug of the past, to awaken in you a sense of life's fragileness, to lead you to glimpse—if even for a moment—the dim figures that once moved in radiance across the background of time.

TIME SCALE

B.C.

15000 — Caves painted at Altamira and Lascaux

3500

Birth of civilization in Egypt and Mesopotamia

3000

Great Pyramid built at Giza

2500

Indus Valley civilization flourishes

Sumerian city of Ur prospers under Third Dynasty

2000

1500 — Minoan civilization flourishes on Crete

Death of Mummy 1770; Volcano on Thera erupts

Death of Tutankhamun

Greek warriors capture Troy

1000

Height of Etruscan civilization

500
—
    Golden Age of Greece
—
—
—
    First Emperor of China; Great Wall is built
—
—
—
    Roman Empire begins; Jesus is born during reign of Augustus
A.D.
—
    Jesus crucified; Dead Sea Scrolls hidden; Masada falls;
—
        Vesuvius buries Pompeii
—
    Catacombs begin in Rome
—
—
    Classic age of Mayan civilization begins
—
    Danish bog burials
—
    Fall of Rome
500
    King Arthur reigns in Britain
—
—
    Oldest datable monument built on Easter Island;
—
        Burial at Sutton Hoo
—
—
—
1000
—
—
—
    Shroud of Turin is first mentioned
—
    Spanish discovery of America
1500
—
    Cortés conquers the Aztec Empire; Pizarro conquers the Incas
—
—
    Jamestown colony founded
—
—
—
—
2000

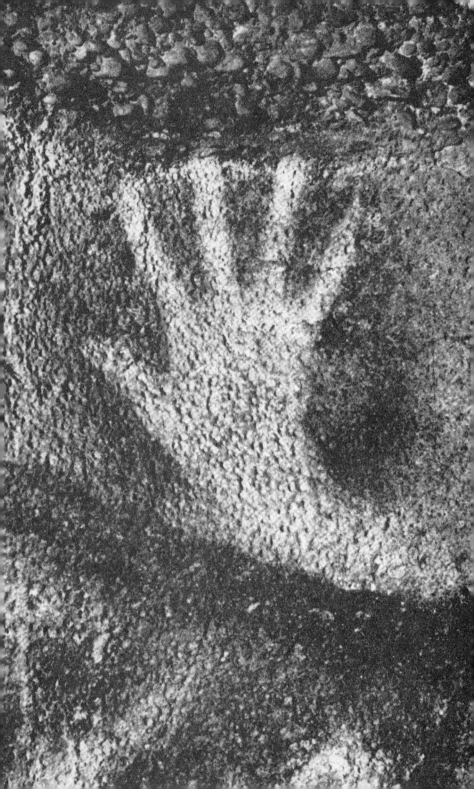

1

Paintings from Prehistory

Thunder from the Cave

FOR A HUNDRED CENTURIES no sound had echoed from the depth of the cave. On the dark walls the hooves of prehistoric beasts hung silent. Herd raced crosswise against herd, a stampede frozen in a glacier of time. Woolly mammoth and wild horse, charging bison and fleet reindeer all held their places on the painted walls just as they had stood when the race was stopped seventeen thousand years before.

Ancient hands had once painted the scene. The mark of the hands was there, outlined by paint on the rock as the artist's sign, five fingers spread, silhouetted in black and red. These were the hands that had hammered flakes from flint to make sharp edges that could kill, the wooden-shafted blades that sang through the air when hurled from the hunter's arm, that plunged into neck and flank of running deer and brought them down. These were the hands that first made the fearsome magic that blazed from the darkness, that scorched the flesh. For ten millennia and more the embers had cooled, but soot still edged the scattered stone lamps where fires once had blazed. Elsewhere were the women carved of stone, recumbent in their pregnancy, bulging with fecundity, large-breasted,

Outline of a prehistoric human hand from the cavern of Pech-Merle, France.

wide-hipped, the faceless givers of young hunters to strengthen the tribe.

*   *   *   *

A little girl came upon them first. She was only five years old, too small for the great herds to even notice. No holder of the singing blade that killed, no hunter she. Her name was Maria, and her father had decided to take her on a great adventure, an outing to the great cave near their home. The place: Altamira, near the northern coast of Spain; the year: 1879.

Slowly the two stepped from daylight into darkness and walked hand in hand with a lamp to guide them. A hundred feet into the cave they heard the deep echo of their voices and found themselves in a great cavernous hall. Following the flickering lamplight, Maria raised her eyes upward toward the dimly lit ceiling, and then she saw them, saw them peering from the darkness, the images of huge painted bulls, radiant in oranges and yellows, in reds and browns. As her father held the lamp higher, the walls echoed with the muted thunder of a thousand hooves.

The cave reached back eight hundred feet and still farther back into humanity's beginnings. Here was the dark sanctuary, illuminated once by prehistoric torchlight, where humans had worshiped the potent beasts whose flesh gave them life. Here young males had been led, millennia before Maria, down the savage passage to manhood's rites, their skin stained with blood-red dye.

In 1940 at Lascaux, in southwest France, two adventurous boys were to make a similar journey into the dark. There they discovered a corridor to a subterranean amphitheater. On its painted rocky ceiling were huge beasts, the biggest a bull eighteen feet in length.

*   *   *   *

Since the discoveries at Altamira and Lascaux, more than one hundred fifty caves have been found in Europe, adorned with the world's earliest art.

Some murals have been found at the entrances of caves or under overhangs, but most are hidden in the depths of caves. Some works were executed in spacious corridors or easily accessible rooms, near or far from daylight. Others —the majority—were produced under extraordinary conditions, hundreds of yards from the entrance, beyond whirlpools or difficult passageways, in recesses where the artist had to work from a prone position, in spiraling tunnels where he had to crawl like a cat and inch his way upward like a chimney-sweep.[3]

We see the scenes through the hunter's eye: the running herd, the darting spear. Invisible behind us is the hunter himself, crouched in dark ambush. Only once does he step forth, portrayed as the archer bending the bow.

Here to these caverns the young male would have come before venturing out to brave his first kill. Here he would have seen the hallowed trophies of his tribe. And in such caverns the young female would have clutched the pregnant icon carved of stone, praying to grow with child.

The bodies of these prehistoric people have been found, their skeletons curled sideways in graves as in sleep, but the dreams that once surged through their fossil skulls are gone. Drawn from the substance of their weapons and tools, the term *Stone Age* is as much a testament to our ignorance of their inner lives as it is a description of their technology. Between the emergence of *Homo sapiens* and the invention of writing, twenty-seven thousand years or more were to pass; between these events fifteen hundred unrecorded generations struggled and died. We have only what survives: a pattern of fingers streaked across the clay of a cave wall, a painted hand silhouetted in the cavernous night. These are the earliest signatures of the human race.

2

The Civilization of Sumer

A Distant Lyre

SHE WOULD BE LATE for the funeral. She knew that now as she hurried down the clay-paved street, hedged by walls of sun-dried brick, winding its way down from the palace to the city's edge.

For days the city of Ur had been in mourning, ever since the death of the king whose body, surrounded by the possessions that had been his in life, now rested on his bier.

Finally she reached the grave site. She hurried down the sloping ramp to the burial pit, past the royal guards with their shimmering spears, past the singers of songs and the harpists with lyres cradled in their arms, to the station where the other ladies of the court, gowned in bright red wool, hair entwined in ribbons of silver and gold, had already gathered in rows beside the burial chamber for the final rites. She found the open place her friends had saved for her and stepped in, exchanging nervous smiles with her peers to either side.

Had she forgotten anything? Was everything in its proper place for the long journey she was to take?

Already the priests had begun to intone the ancient hymn. Slowly, in hushed dignity, they bore in their hands the cup of fate and paused for each to drink down its sleep-giving liquid.

The jewelry of Queen Pu-abi of Ur.

Soon weariness overtook her, a heaviness descending on her limbs until she slumped to the ground.

It was only when all were asleep, sleeping their endless sleep, that the weeping began among the mourners gathered above. They mourned for the king and his beloved wife, for his musicians and beloved entertainer, for his beloved valet and his household, and for the beloved caretaker who lay with him in that place, even for the girl so forgetful who had hurried to her final sleep, rushing to eternity.

*   *   *   *

Between the valley of the Tigris and Euphrates and north of the Persian Gulf, in a "land between the rivers" called Mesopotamia in antiquity and southern Iraq today, there arose one of the earliest civilizations—according to some, the very first to emerge. Here, not long before 3000 B.C., a fertile soil vitalized by ample water permitted farmers to grow wheat in such abundance that surpluses came to exist. The need for well-maintained canals to direct the river waters and for dikes to restrain recurrent floods demanded a strong government. The need to store and distribute grain for a large and growing population fostered both organization and bureaucracy, and out of the necessity for calculation and record keeping mathematical notation began. Writing was invented, with symbols for ideas—and later, sounds—pressed by wedge-shaped styluses into lumps of riverbank clay. A religious awe of the heavens coupled with a keen awareness of celestial change led to the development of astronomy, and on lofty stepped platforms, made of brick and called *ziggurats,* the people raised their temples to the gods. Their system of measuring space and time, based on the numbers 6, 10, and 60, govern our lives even now in the 360-degree circle, the 24-hour day, and the 60-minute hour. We measure out our lives in the rhythms of vanished Sumeria.

Unlike the Nile, the waters of the Tigris and Euphrates were unpredictable. Flooding could be sudden and disastrous, inundating entire communities and covering them in several feet of mud. Memories of such floods were enshrined in Mesopotamia's poetry as a single great disaster from which a Sumerian Noah emerged. Also unlike the Nile, the rivers of Mesopotamia could change their course over the centuries, removing life-giving water and commerce. Eventually, a city would be abandoned, becoming what the Arabs later would call a *tell,* a deserted mound of layered ruins piled up by centuries-long occupation and reoccupation of the same site.

Whipped by sandstorms, their gray or yellow skin scarred by broken bricks and shattered pottery, such tells became the province of the hawk, the jackal, and the wolf. Only the mutilated temple tower, blunted archetype for the Bible's Tower of Babel, testified to the former glory of Ur, once the queen of Sumeria's cities.

Yet in the right light, to the right observer, Ur even in its ruined state could evoke the image of a time when a curious and energetic people lived bright lives beneath a warming sky, when the Euphrates flowed closely by, when the water of canals shimmered in the sun, and the land was golden with wheat. "I fell in love with Ur," one modern visitor wrote, "with its beauty in the evenings, the ziggurat standing up, faintly shadowed, and that wide sea of sand with its lovely pale colours of apricot, rose, blue, and mauve, changing every minute."[4]

The year was 1930: the visitor, mystery writer Agatha Christie. Pained by recent divorce, she had journeyed to distant Ur to visit the new excavations and to seek fresh experiences. Her hosts would be Leonard Woolley and his wife Katherine. Woolley, a master of organization and detail, headed the joint British–American dig at Ur.

The rediscovery of Ur had begun in 1854 when the British vice-consul at Basra, J. E. Taylor, commissioned by the British Museum to explore Mesopotamian ruins, was drawn to the most prominent tell in all Iraq, the one Arabs called Tell el Muqayyar from the Arabic word for asphalt, the petroleum resin used by ancient inhabitants to cement together their ziggurat's bricks. Inscriptions found by Taylor in the only recently deciphered cuneiform script identified the city as Ur, a name that recalled Ur of the Chaldees, the home of the biblical patriarch Abraham.

Later explorations were eagerly followed up by Woolley when he was named director of a British Museum–University of Pennsylvania expedition in 1922. Woolley, whose father had been a minister and who himself had earlier considered a theological career, hoped to reveal more of Ur's story. Later, Agatha Christie would meet and marry Woolley's assistant, Max Mallowan, himself destined for a distinguished career in archaeology as excavator of the Assyrian cities of Nimrud and Nineveh.

Digging toward the base of Ur's mound, Woolley was to find a startling confirmation of the Bible. As he penetrated down through a layer containing very early Sumerian artifacts, he came upon virgin soil, normally a sign to the archeologist that a bottom line has been reached beneath which there is no further evidence of human habitation. But to Woolley's eye, the level of the virgin soil was unnaturally high above the surrounding plain, and so he ordered his laborers to continue digging. Three, four, five, six, seven, eight feet of barren mud, and then—suddenly—artifacts once more! But artifacts of a different kind: above the mud level, examples of metal tools and wheel-made pottery; below, traces of a simpler culture that lacked such technologies.

Woolley himself was convinced of what the virgin soil meant, but wanted to see if others agreed. When he asked his wife Katherine what she thought, she casually remarked, "Well, of course, it's the Flood."

It was a flood indeed, and one that had caused a radical interruption in Ur's early history. Although it was tempting to think of it as evidence of *the* Flood of Genesis, a comparative study of mud levels at other Sumerian sites showed Woolley that the flood that had destroyed Ur in the distant past had not drowned all of Sumer's cities. Yet it was certainly the kind of catastrophe that would have inspired the notion of a universal destruction.

Gold beads emerged from Woolley's trial excavations in Ur's cemetery, but the scientist in him restrained the romantic: he would let four years pass before returning to the site of potential treasure, sufficient time to allow him and his crew to gain the experience necessary to extract every bit of information the cemetery would yield. For that was Woolley's goal: information. "Our object," he was to assert, "was to get history, not to fill museum cases with miscellaneous curios."[5]

Woolley clearly recognized the inherent paradox of archaeology: However much it may be motivated by the search for knowledge, excavation is necessarily destructive. For evidence in lower levels to be uncovered, upper strata must be obliterated. Thus, unless the location of each object disinterred is carefully recorded, and its position relative to all other finds precisely detailed, it will be impossible to reconstruct the cultural fabric of which it was a part, let alone its own place in time.

So it was not until 1926 that Woolley turned back to the cemetery. Ironically, the inhabitants of Ur had buried their bodies and treasures in a rubbish heap. In a community where living space was limited to the top surface of a mound, even a dump would be utilized, especially if it happened to be situated not far from the city's sacred compound containing a palace and shrines.

Woolley's diggings were to reveal over two thousand simple graves. In one such grave, at the bottom of a four- to twelve-foot shaft, the skeleton lay resting on its right side as though in sleep, often within traces of a humble coffin. Impressions remained in the earth of the reed mat that had served as the bed or the lining of the grave. Objects of less perishable material were also found, possessions the deceased had once owned and would keep for all eternity— jewelry (sometimes of gold), a drinking cup, perhaps a protective knife.

Near the very end of the first digging season in the cemetery, Woolley came upon the richest of the individual graves, one that contained a helmet that he would later regard as the single most beautiful object to be unearthed at Ur. Beside the waist of Mes-kalam-dug (his name was found inscribed on his seal) traces of silver were still visible where a silver belt had once held a still-glistening golden dagger and its whetstone of blue lapis lazuli suspended from a golden ring. On his skull was a work of extraordinary beauty, a helmet of gold, expertly shaped in the form of a wig, with locks of hair curling down at the sides and tied in a bun at the back. Even ears had been modeled with holes in them to allow this ancient leader to hear as well as to command. His vanity was marked by the inclusion in the grave of a skin-care kit of gold, which contained a pencil, lancet, and tweezers.

Later, beneath the private graves, Woolley found elaborate royal burial chambers, remarkable for the wealth of objects they contained, but all the more extraordinary because they constituted mass burials in which guardians and servants had been interred with their masters in order to join them in the next world. Their poses, and the absence of visible wounds, suggested the use of a sleeping potion or gentle poison. Evidence was also found of ceremonial sacrifices and funeral feasts made on the beaten earth used to cover the sepulcher.

Altogether, Woolley found the graves of sixteen kings and queens of Ur who had reigned during the middle of the third millennium B.C., the age when Egypt's fourth dynasty pharaohs were building their pyramids at Giza. Just as the tombs of the pharaohs would be robbed, so would these graves at Ur, by ancient thieves who broke into the tombs from above, sometimes while digging later graves. Of the sixteen royal tombs, only two were found intact. Yet even in the ransacked tombs the thieves had not been thorough.

In one violated grave, ineffectually guarded by spear-carrying skeletons with flattened copper helmets on their crushed skulls, a king lay in state. Beside his burial-chamber wall had stood nine women; their skeletons now lay on the floor, derelict except for the ornate headdresses they still wore: golden flower petals once poised over their heads, and over their foreheads a fringe of golden beech-leaves and beads of lapis lazuli and orange-red carnelian. From their ears had hung large earrings of beaten gold in the shape of crescent moons.

By the ramp at the head of the funeral cortege were the remains of two ox-drawn four-wheeled wagons, the oldest wheeled vehicles that have ever been discovered. In the collapsed tomb, the grain in the wheels' wood was impressed in the heavy earth, and traces of the beaded reins and leather tires could still be seen. Two lyres were also in the tomb, their sounding-boxes animated by metal bulls' heads.

When queen Pu-abi had neared death, she had asked that she be buried close to her husband. A shaft was dug down and her crypt was prepared over the site of her husband's grave. Near her grasping hand was a golden cup. Beneath an elaborate headdress, her hair had been looped with delicate golden ribbon. Beads of gold, silver, lapis lazuli, carnelian, agate, and chalcedony still clung like a collar around her neck. Her gown had disintegrated, but the golden amulets that had once decorated it now lay beside her, alongside shells filled with green eye shadow.

Pu-abi's eternally idle hours would be spent playing a royal parlor game on a board inlaid with shell in floral and domino patterns, equipped with carved tokens for two players. It was one of two such games found by Woolley in the Royal Graves but, alas, without instructions on how to play. As the queen played, she could sip a refreshing drink from a golden straw buried with her and listen to the strains of a nearby lyre. Although the wooden body of the lyre had decomposed, plaster of paris poured into the imprint left in the earth allowed for its later reconstruction.

In yet another of the royal graves an object was found bearing a portrait of Sumerian civilization more revealing than any other single artifact. Called the "Royal Standard of Ur," it was found resting beside the skeleton of a man, capped in lapis lazuli beads, who had once held it in his hands during the funeral ceremony. Discovered by Woolley in thousands of pieces and painstakingly reassembled, the two-sided mosaic was composed of bits of white shell, blue lapis lazuli, and pink limestone arranged and glued with asphalt to a wooden backing.

Reconstructed, the mosaics show back-to-back scenes of

war and the celebration of victory. In multiple registers, columns of Sumerian infantrymen march to battle on one side, while donkey-drawn chariots course over the fallen bodies of the enemy. On the opposite side, prisoners of war and captured livestock are paraded past seated fleece-skirted leaders of Ur, who are drinking beer as they listen to a musician play the lyre.

In the largest burial of all, the so-called "Great Death Pit," Woolley found the remains of six armed guards and sixty-eight women. Four of the women held harps, the hands of one musician still resting where the strings had been. Twenty-eight women had worn golden ribbons in their hair. The others had worn ribbons of another metal, as Woolley could deduce from the faint traces of a purplish powder—silver chloride—on their skulls. Of all ancient metals, gold endures best, but silver, if it is not thick or protected from soil acids, will turn to dust.

As Woolley knelt beside one of the skeletons, a gray, flat disk—about three inches across and lying about level with her waist—caught his eye. Later that evening, cleaning and inspecting it by lamplight in his excavation headquarters, he saw what it was.

> It was the silver hair-ribbon, but it had never been worn —carried apparently in the woman's pocket, it was just as she had taken it from her room, done up in a tight coil with the ends brought over to prevent its coming undone; and since it formed thus a comparatively solid mass of metal and had been protected by the cloth of her dress, it was very well preserved and even the delicate edges of the ribbon were sharply distinct. Why the owner had not put it on one could not say; perhaps she was late for the ceremony and had not time to dress properly.[6]

"Perhaps she was late. . . ." And what was she thinking, that anxious royal servant, as she hurried to her sleep so long ago? What had her last thoughts been as she felt herself grow weary and saw the strung lyre tumble slowly into Sumer's dust?

In the depth of the night, as the archaeologist turned off his bedside lamp and plunged himself into darkness, a breeze stirred outside, swirling through the trenches of Ur like the current of an ancient river, like the current of time itself.

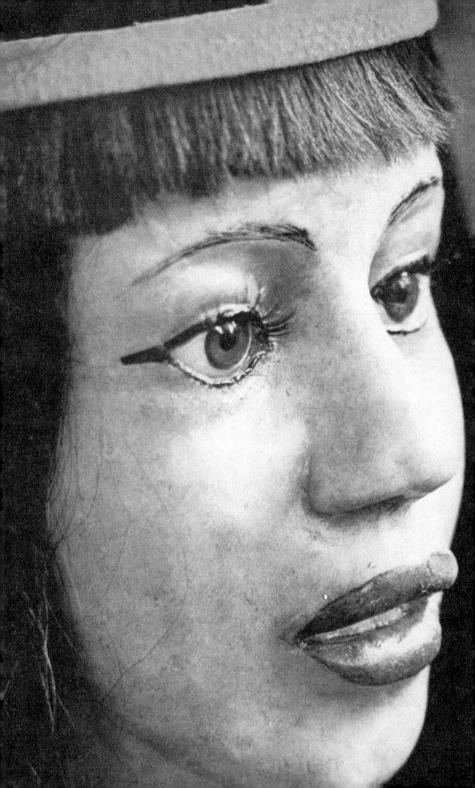

3

The Mummies of Egypt

Voices from the Tomb

SHE LAY on the operating table, her eyes still open, staring upward. Methodically, the surgeons removed the bandages. Her legs were taut and stiff; her arms lay crosswise on her chest. She no longer breathed but the surgeons worked on, cutting deeper through the depths of dark-stained linen as though somehow her life could be found again, retrieved. Her gilded cheeks still shone, radiant beneath the ceiling lights of the operating theater. How like the light of another sun her face had known, been warmed by once, thousands of miles away, more than a million noons ago along the Nile.

* * * *

In Egypt the sun almost always shines. To the people of ancient Egypt the sun was a life-giving god whose setting in the west and daily rebirth in the east held out to them the promise of their own resurrection. It was in the west, the horizon of the sun's setting, that the Egyptians dug their cemeteries and built their tombs, in the western desert beyond the fertile green ribbon of the Nile.

In such hot, dry sands, bodies deposited in shallow burials are naturally preserved, for the body's desiccation inhibits

The reconstructed face of Mummy 1770.

the action of bacteria that would otherwise cause its decay. Uncovered by sandstorms, such naturally preserved bodies confirmed in the hearts of the living the hope of eternal life, for if the body might survive for centuries, why not the soul?

Such shallow burials, however, incurred risk. Trusting in an afterlife, the Egyptians buried their loved ones' possessions in the grave, believing these objects could be used and enjoyed in the life to come. There were others, however, who did not hesitate to violate the sanctity of a grave in order to enrich their own lives. Such thieves readily penetrated the shallow sands to find treasure.

To guard against such thefts and to ensure a secure afterlife for the souls of their loved ones, the pious Egyptians dug deeper graves. But in so doing they endangered the survival of the body itself, for at lower depths, where the sun's heat cannot reach, moisture fosters decay. Were the body to decompose, the soul would no longer have a home, and all hope of an afterlife would end. To solve their spiritual dilemma, the ancient Egyptians devised a means of artificially protecting the body against decay to enable the deep storage of the body and its possessions.

Just as the Egyptians are silent about how they built the pyramids, so are they silent as to their methods of embalming the dead, probably because embalming was a sacred craft. Only one fragmentary scroll speaks of the stages by which a body was preserved. For more information, we must turn from Egyptian records to the writings of an ancient Greek—Herodotus, the "father of history," who lived during the fifth century B.C., the Golden Age of Athens. Herodotus went to Egypt to gather information for a history book he was writing. On his visit he spoke with the Egyptians about their land and culture. Though his research was conducted at a time when the art of embalming had declined, the information he presents is valuable because it is based on interviews with Egyptians familiar with ancestral ways.

Herodotus relates that there were three classes of embalming. The type selected depended on the wealth of the deceased. The treatment of the body did not reflect mere ostentation but had profound consequences: the better the body was preserved, the surer the guarantee of immortality.

Here then is Herodotus's account in all its graphic detail:

The mode of embalming, according to the most perfect process, is the following: they take first a crooked piece of iron, and with it draw out the brain through the nostrils, thus getting rid of a portion, while the skull is cleared of the rest by rinsing with drugs; next they make a cut along the flank with a sharp Ethiopian stone, and take out the whole contents of the abdomen, which they then cleanse, washing it thoroughly with palm-wine, and again frequently with an infusion of pounded aromatics. After this they fill the cavity with the purest bruised myrrh, with cassia, and every other sort of spicery except frankincense, and sew up the opening. Then the body is placed in natron for seventy days, and covered entirely over. After the expiration of that space of time, which must not be exceeded, the body is washed, and wrapped round, from head to foot, with bandages of fine linen cloth, smeared over with gum, which is used generally by the Egyptians in the place of glue, and in this state it is given back to the relations, who enclose it in a wooden case which they have had made for the purpose, shaped into the figure of a man. Then fastening the case, they place it in a sepulchral chamber, upright against the wall. Such is the most costly way of embalming the dead.

If persons wish to avoid expense, and choose the second process, the following is the method pursued: syringes are filled with oil made from the cedar-tree, which is then, without any incision or disembowelling, injected into the bowel. The passage is stopped, and the body laid in natron the prescribed number of days. At the end of the time the cedar-oil is allowed to make its escape: and such is its power that it brings with it the whole stomach and intestines in a liquid state. The natron meanwhile has dissolved the flesh, and so nothing is left of the dead body but the skin and the bones. It is returned in this condition to the relatives, without any further trouble being bestowed upon it.

The third method of embalming, which is practised in the case of the poorer classes, is to clear out the intestines with a purge, and let the body lie in natron the seventy days, after which it is at once given to those who come to fetch it away.[7]

From Herodotus's account we see that the basis of Egyptian embalming was the dehydration of the body through chemical means, aided by the prior removal of bodily organs. (The heart was not removed, as it was looked upon as the seat of consciousness.) The drying agent the Egyptians used—Herodotus calls it *natron*—was a locally available natural salt compound resembling bicarbonate of soda. In addition to its drying properties, this crystalline substance was a powerful degreaser that helped eliminate much of the fat from the corpse. When the corpse was dried out, it was stuffed with rags or sawdust to give it a more lifelike appearance. Onions and garlic, which have antibacterial and fungicidal properties, were sometimes added to the stuffing.

The *gum* that was smeared over the bandages became the source of our word *mummy,* for, later, when Arab onlookers saw the blackish resin, they called it (and the corpse it covered) *mummia,* their own word for bitumen or tar.

Mummification and burial were only the first steps in securing immortality for the soul. The soul, or *ka,* still had to make the perilous journey to the kingdom of Osiris, divine king of the dead. On this journey the *ka* was aided by a hieroglyphic guidebook, the *Book of the Dead,* placed with it in the tomb. After the *ka* was interrogated and swore its moral purity before a divine tribunal, its heart was weighed in a set of balance-scales against the ostrich feather of truth. If the heart was as light as a feather (that is, pure of heart), the soul was granted the sensual joys of the afterlife for all eternity. If the heart failed this ancient lie-detector test, the soul was swallowed up by an infernal monster.

To ensure the morally pure soul an eternal home in the event the body should ever decay, images of the deceased were carved out of stone and placed in the tomb or were painted on the tomb walls. The presence of a *cartouche*, the name of the deceased painted or inscribed in hieroglyphs, provided additional eternal life-insurance. Yet the mummy, safeguarded by coffin, sarcophagus, and tomb, remained the soul's primary home.

The tombs of Egypt are like time capsules; the mummies, encapsulated voyagers from another world. However, we must not conclude from their preoccupation with death that the Egyptians were obsessed by it. Rather, they were obsessed with life, devoting their every energy to its continuation. In reaching for that immortality the Egyptians gained one they could not have imagined, for their abiding faith in an afterlife generated everlasting works by which they have come to live in our minds. If the mummies of Egypt are voyagers from another time, what message do they bear us and how may we interpret it?

The wordless message of the mummies resides in their very bodies. Museums, which house mummies today, may cause us to forget that the mummy itself is a veritable museum, a "biologic museum."[8] Mummies can show us graphically what the ancient Egyptians looked like. We can assess their average life span, deduce their diet (and its effects upon their health), determine the maladies they were afflicted by, and diagnose the causes of their death.

Mummies can also teach us about animal life in ancient Egypt, for animals were embalmed as well. Because certain creatures were associated with deities (some Egyptian gods even had animal heads), such animals were regarded as sacred. Mummified remains have been found of crocodiles, cobras, and baboons, of birds such as the ibis and falcon, of cats and dogs, and even of a pet gerbil, embalmed and buried with a sack of food for its use in the netherworld.

Shortly after its invention in 1895, X-ray photography was applied to the study of Egyptian mummies. This nondestructive technique permitted mummies to be examined without their having to be unwrapped. At its inception, however, X-ray photography was a cumbersome process and pictures lacked sharp resolution.

In the 1960s the radiological examination of mummies was reactivated under the leadership of Dr. James E. Harris, a professor of orthodontics at the University of Michigan. Dr. Harris and his colleagues realized that the teeth of Egypt's mummies could form a useful data base against which to measure the condition of teeth in modern Egypt and the existence of dental problems in Egypt today.

The results of the Michigan team's investigations were fascinating and, in some cases, unexpected. The ancient Egyptians, for example, do not seem to have been bothered by cavities for most of their history. Only when Egypt was conquered by the Greeks and Romans—and Egypt's diet became sweeter and stickier—did decay become a problem. Instead, Egyptians were plagued for most of their history by dental attrition, the wearing down of tooth surfaces, and attendant complications. The Michigan researchers concluded that such attrition could be attributed to the regular presence of sand in Egyptian food—in part windblown from the desert, in part deliberately added to wheat during milling to help make flour finer.

The X-ray studies also revealed the hitherto unknown presence of amulets and jewelry beneath the wrappings of some mummies. The X rays of two bodies, rewrapped by priests in ancient times, showed the handiwork of thieves: baubles, bangles, and beads still scattered in disarray and a body so mangled by greed that copper wire was later needed to hold it together.

In addition to radiological examination, mummies have also been unwrapped and autopsied. Tissue samples have been taken from mummies and analyzed by pathologists searching for evidence of ancient disease. Light and electron microscopes have been employed and sophisticated chemical tests performed. The work of these palaeopathologists (specialists in the study of ancient disease) has demonstrated the presence in ancient Egypt of many maladies: circulatory conditions such as high blood pressure, hardening of the arteries, and heart attack; respiratory conditions such as bronchitis and pneumonia; gallstones, kidney stones, and severe appendicitis; arthritis and slipped discs; smallpox; parasitic infestation; a punctured eardrum; and even gout. In many cases, the investigators have been able to describe the very symptoms the subject would have manifested in the years, months, or days before his or her death.

Surgical gowns, masks, and gloves must be worn during such autopsies. These precautions reduce the possibility that microorganisms from the investigators will contaminate tissue samples taken from the mummy. Such precautions are also intended to protect the investigators themselves: through contact with the mummy or inhalation they could contract the germs of an ancient disease for which their bodies have no natural defense.

*   *   *   *

One of the most intriguing mummy autopsies was performed in 1976 at Manchester University under the direction of Dr. Rosalie David. The mummy in question was known only by its museum catalog number, 1770.

Notwithstanding this impersonal number, 1770 had once been alive, with a name and human emotions. Its humanity was now wrapped in resin-soaked bindings, its face masked beneath a skin of gilded linen, its dark-lined eyes blankly open.

When preliminary X rays were taken, they indicated that 1770 was a girl between thirteen and fourteen years of age. Curiously, the lower parts of her legs seemed to be missing. The X rays also disclosed a strange round mass near her feet.

As the autopsy commenced, the gilded mask was removed. The bones of the skull and neck were found, fractured into thirty pieces; only the upper jaw and face remained intact. Some of the bones were tinged with red and blue paint, a substance that could have only been applied if the flesh had deteriorated before burial.

On each of the fingers that rested over the chest were tubes of gold foil. On the chest itself lay a brightly painted linen cover with golden nipple-covers set over the site of the breasts. The chest cavity was empty; the abdomen and pelvis packed with bandages and mud.

Attached to the outside of the pelvis was a tightly rolled bandage, an artificial phallus meant to ensure virility in the life to come. The corpse had apparently decomposed so badly that the ancient morticians, uncertain of its sex, had bestowed upon it nipple covers *and* an artificial phallus!

When the Manchester team reached the lower extremities, they discovered that the leg bones had been severed: the right leg above the knee, the left leg below. They speculated that 1770 had been crushed by falling masonry and was buried for a time in rubble, or that she had drowned in the Nile and had been chewed by a crocodile or hippopotamus.

Faced with the predicament of preparing an incomplete body for burial, the morticians constructed false legs out of reeds and mud and attached them to the remaining bone, adding artificial feet with gilded nail covers and decorative slippers—the curious mass that had shown up on the X rays where the feet should have been.

In the mummy wrappings were found ancient insects (flies and beetles), and in the abdominal wall of the mummy itself were the calcified remains of a large parasitical Guinea-worm.

Although 1770's skull had shattered into many fragments, it was possible to reconstruct it and even to attempt a hypothetical facial reconstruction in wax based upon the average depth of soft tissue on the human face and the information 1770's skull and teeth could give about her facial contours. Given false eyelashes and glass eyes of warm brown, fitted with an Egyptian-style wig, and made up with traditional cosmetics, the face of 1770 emerged, the face of a lovely Egyptian girl just entering her teens, whose life had violently ended.

But when had she lived? In what period of Egypt's long history?

To get these answers, scientists subjected samples of her flesh and bandages to carbon-14 analysis. This dating technique is based on the fact that all organic material contains carbon. Part of this carbon is a radioactive isotope called carbon-14. As long as anything organic has life, the proportion between its radioactive and nonradioactive carbon is constantly maintained. But when something dies, it begins to lose this radioactivity at a rate that is fixed and measurable. After about fifty-six hundred years, for example, half of its radioactivity is gone.

When organic materials are found by archaeologists, a sample can be sent to a laboratory for radioactive analysis. The sample is first burned. Then the resultant carbon-dioxide gas is purified and studied to determine how much radioactivity remains. From this measurement, technicians can estimate the approximate age of the sample and of the source from which it came.

Such tests performed on tissue samples from mummy 1770 showed that she had died sometime between 1600 and 1250 B.C. But identical tests performed on her bandages showed *they* dated between A.D. 105 and 405. Thus her body had been wrapped well over a thousand years after she had died.

What could explain such a gap in time? Why had 1770 been given such treatment so long after her death? And why would priests wrap a body so badly decomposed that even its sex was obscured?

The answer may lie in Egyptian religion. Herodotus tells us that the body of anyone who died in the sacred Nile was looked upon as sacred too.

> Whensoever any one, Egyptian or foreigner, has lost his life by falling prey to a crocodile, or by drowning in the river, the law compels the inhabitants of the city near which the body is cast up to have it embalmed, and to bury it in one of the sacred repositories with all possible magnificence. No one may touch the corpse, not even any of the friends or relatives, but only the priests of the Nile, who prepare it for burial with their own hands—regarding it as something more than the mere body of a man—and themselves lay it in the tomb.[9]

If 1770 died in the Nile, her body could have decomposed badly before it was found. Pious priests would have then embalmed her and restored her legs. Centuries later, other priests could have ceremonially rewrapped the sacred body to keep it well preserved.

But who was the girl that 1770 once had been, the brown-eyed girl who lived beside the green Nile a million noons ago? 1770—what was your name?

*   *   *   *

Young 1770's hope, and the hope of all ancient Egyptians, was to be reborn after death. That hope may yet be fulfilled by the science of genetic engineering. In the process known as cloning, the chromosomes of a donor cell are implanted into an ovum from which all chromosomes have been removed. In normal sexual reproduction, the chromosomes of the sperm (half the number necessary for conception) join the chromosomes of the ovum, completing a set. The individual born of this union reflects the pooled genetic characteristics of ovum and sperm. In cloning, however, an already complete set of chromosomes is removed from a donor cell and is transplanted intact into an ovum from which the nucleus has been removed. The result of this process is the birth of an individual that is an exact replica of the donor.

Although for a long time the process of cloning seemed to belong chiefly to the realm of science fiction, the cloning of lower animals—frogs, for example—has already been achieved in the laboratory. Technical obstacles block the cloning of humans. Yet even if these problems are solved, ethical considerations staggering in proportion will still remain: Have we the right to replicate certain human types? Should we redesign, through genetic manipulation, the creatures we make? And what may the consequences of our actions be?

For Egyptologists another question will remain: Should science clone a mummy?

The structure of chromosomal architecture is extremely fragile: death, desiccation, and time take a heavy toll on the structural survival of DNA, or deoxyribonucleic acid, the substance in which genetic characteristics are encoded. Cloning, however, does not require an original set of chromosomes; a synthetically manufactured copy of the molecular structure, if implanted in a living ovum, will provide a sufficient genetic blueprint for cellular reproduction to proceed.

In 1985 a team of scientists from the University of Uppsala, Sweden, led by Dr. Svante Paabo, extracted and duplicated the genetic material from the skin of a one-year-old boy mummified in Egypt about 400 B.C. Using tissue culture, the Swedish researchers succeeded in growing the boy's genes, the first time DNA has been recovered and duplicated from an ancient biologic source. Their achievement offers the possibility of establishing genetic relationships, not only between mummies but also between living and extinct species, a possibility of profound importance to our understanding of evolution. More immediately and more startlingly, it offers the possibility of cloning an entire mummy.

Inserted into a living ovum and successfully implanted into the uterus of a surrogate mother, the chromosomes of the dead Egyptian donor would reproduce themselves until they were delivered into the world as a newborn infant. Thus a mummy could be reborn, not as one knowing Egypt's ancient language and culture but as the physical and intellectual replica of the baby originally born beside the Nile.

Although scant traces of her flesh remain, 1770 could be offered such an opportunity. Through cloning, she might be reborn to live beyond the age when her ancient life had violently ended, and be given the chance to grow to womanhood. Someday, in the back row of a college classroom she might sit, her brown eyes wide with wonder, learning about a lost world that was once hers.

4

Tutankhamun and His Queen

Behind the Golden Mask

> *I am thy first love, I am thy garden,*
> *Scented with spices, fragrant with flowers.*
> *Deep runs my channel, smoothed by thy tillage,*
> *Cooled by the North Wind, filled by the Nile.* [10]

IF ANYTHING CAN CONVEY the humanness of the past, it is this—an ancient love poem. The sentiments it contains have traveled across three thousand years of history. Yet, despite the distance in time, the poem's content witnesses the feelings we hold in common with those who once lived long ago.

Of all the love poems in the world the oldest are the love poems of ancient Egypt, composed in the second millennium B.C. These poems speak to us of love, the most fragile of all human emotions. They survive because human beings have always felt the impulse to express their inner life in some external form, to give to an invisible spirit material expression. Thus antique passions live on, inked onto now-crumbling papyrus or traced on the shards of vases once whole. If it is marvelous that material artifacts endure from lost civilizations, how much more marvelous it is that human

The golden mask of Tutankhamun at the time of its discovery.

emotions can be faithfully transmitted after thousands of years.

It is the land of Egypt itself that has enabled us to have these poems: on the wet banks of the Nile grew papyrus reeds that were transmuted into the world's oldest paper; in the dry sands of the desert, the scrolls were kept from decay.

Yet it is one thing to possess an ancient scroll; something else to understand its meaning. For almost two thousand years the meaning of hieroglyphics was forgotten until a chance discovery by Napoleon's troops near a delta village called Rosetta. Found in 1799, the Rosetta Stone, as it came to be called, proved to be the key that unlocked the secrets of Egyptian literature.

The Rosetta Stone contained a bilingual inscription, a single message written out in two different languages. At the top were Egyptian hieroglyphics; at the bottom, the same message in Greek. Since ancient Greek could be read and understood, scholars were able to deduce the general meaning of the Egyptian text. By 1822 the Rosetta Stone was completely deciphered, thanks to the insights of English scientist Thomas Young and the labors of French linguist Jean François Champollion.

With the decipherment of hieroglyphic writing and the eventual translation of Egyptian literature, the long-silent Sphinx was finally free to speak. From stories of adventure, bits of wisdom and humor, and erotic verse there emerged the essential humanity of the ancient Egyptian, a humanity that had for too long been hidden behind a veil of mysticism and otherworldliness.

*   *   *   *

In 1922, one hundred years after the Rosetta Stone had been deciphered, an astounding event took place which further altered our perception of ancient Egypt. After searching in vain for five years through the pharaonic graveyard known as the Valley of the Kings, English archaeologist Howard Carter made the most sensational find in the history of archaeology, the discovery of King Tut's tomb.

Carter and his financial backer, Lord Carnarvon, had been searching for the one royal tomb not accounted for in the archaeological record, the tomb of a minor ruler named Tutankhamun. Boy-king at the age of eight, Tutankhamun had come to the throne in the aftermath of religious revolution. His brother, the pharaoh Akhenaton, had taken the radical step of instituting monotheism in Egypt, antagonizing the powerful priesthoods of the land by closing their temples and confiscating their rich estates. In place of the many gods of Egypt, Akhenaton venerated only one, the god Aton, symbolized by the life-giving disc and benevolent rays of the sun. Following a philosophy of love, Akhenaton encouraged a new spirit of tender naturalism in Egyptian art, a spirit present in affectionate family portraits of the pharaoh, his beautiful queen, Nefertiti, and their daughters.

But Akhenaton's tenderness, when transferred to foreign policy, only acted to antagonize Egypt's military establishment in what had heretofore been an age of expansive imperialism. When Akhenaton died, the religious and military hierarchy sought out a legitimate heir who could become the instrument by which the old ways might be reestablished. They even convinced him to change his name from Tutankh*aton* to Tutankh*amun* in order to symbolize the restored primacy of Amun, god of the Egyptian state.

Tutankhamun's reign was brief: he died in 1352 B.C. at the age of eighteen or nineteen with no notable accomplishments; but he lived during the most glorious period of Egyptian history, the 18th dynasty. Surely, thought Carter and Carnarvon, if his tomb could be found, it would reflect the splendor of that age. Yet apart from some remnants of his funeral—floral wreaths and common vases found in a pit—no material trace of his death had ever been uncovered.

On November 4, 1922, while excavating beneath the rough foundations of an ancient work camp, Carter's men came upon a step cut into the bedrock of the valley floor, the first of sixteen buried steps that led down to a sealed doorway bearing Tutankhamun's name. Beyond the sealed doorway was a rubble-filled passageway and beyond that a second sealed door. Carter prepared to enter the tomb.

> Slowly, desperately slowly it seemed to us as we watched, the debris that encumbered the lower part of the doorway was removed, until at last we had the whole door clear before us. The decisive moment had arrived. With trembling hands I made a tiny breach in the upper-lefthand corner. Darkness and blank space, as far as an iron testing rod could reach, showed that whatever lay beyond was empty. Candle tests were applied as a precaution against possible foul gases, and then, widening the hole a little, I inserted the candle and peered in, Lord Carnarvon, Lady Evelyn, and [my assistant] Callender standing anxiously beside me to hear the verdict. At first I could see nothing —the hot air escaping from the chamber caused the candle flame to flicker—but presently, as my eyes grew accustomed to the light, details of the room within emerged slowly from the mist: strange animals, statues, and gold— everywhere the glint of gold. For the moment—an eternity it must have seemed to the others—I was struck dumb with amazement, and when Lord Carnarvon, unable to stand the suspense any longer, inquired anxiously, "Can you see anything?" it was all I could do to get out the words, "Yes, wonderful things." Widening the hole a little farther so that we could both see, we inserted an electric torch.[11]

The tomb Carter was to enter was crammed with almost five thousand objects, mostly personal possessions placed in the tomb so that they might accompany the pharaoh into the spirit world and brighten his days. For Tutankhamun's delight there were perfumes jarred in alabaster (including a pine-scented after-shave lotion) and labeled cannisters of roast duck and veal (the meat all properly embalmed so it would last forever). Packed away for his comfort were ostrich feather fans to cool him, pairs of gold-tooled slippers, and the Egyptian version of the pillow, a curved neck rest of stone. Game boards (for a game like Parchesi) were provided to help him while away his leisure hours. For more active pursuits, chariots were garaged in the tomb, their parts neatly stacked up, awaiting reassembly in the spirit world. Souvenirs of Tutankhamun's childhood were there too: a child-sized chair of ebony and ivory (just a bit over two feet tall) and the model boats he had fashioned as a boy, boats that would now magically transport his soul across the heavenly ocean to the western horizon where the god Osiris waited to greet him.

Inside a crypt the body of Tutankhamun rested in a brown quartzite sarcophagus carved with the images of protective goddesses, their arms lovingly outstretched. Within the sarcophagus were four interlocking coffins, the first three of gilded wood, the innermost of one-eighth-inch-thick 22-carat gold. Inside, with face and shoulders encased in a golden portrait mask, was Tutankhamun's linen-swathed mummy, encrusted in golden jewelry and amulets. A gold-bladed dagger had been laid by his side for protection. The petals of spring floral wreaths, tenderly placed over his corpse more than three thousand Aprils ago, still lay intact.

Perhaps *she* had placed them there—Ankhesenamun, his queen—for she too lives on in the tomb, through images of graciousness and quiet affection and through hieroglyphs that caption her acts of reverent love: "Ankhesenamun, the Great Royal Wife, beloved of the Great Enchantress, the Heiress, Great of Favors, Mistress of Upper and Lower Egypt, Lady of Graciousness, Sweet of Love, the Great Wife whom he loves, Lady of the Two Lands."[12]

Symbols of their marriage contract are contained in an alabaster box: two locks of hair wrapped in linen beside an ivory pomegranate, symbol of fertility. But Tutankhamun was not her first husband. Years earlier, when she was only a little girl, she had been made to marry her own father, Akhenaton. Why had this happened?

In ancient Egypt the royal bloodline was traced through the female. Estranged from his wife Nefertiti, Akhenaton had chosen to marry one of their daughters as a way of protecting the legitimacy of his reign. Thus, for reasons of state, father and daughter were wed.

When Akhenaton died, Ankhesenamun was given in marriage again, this time (at perhaps age eleven or twelve) to Tutankhamun, himself then only an eight- or nine-year-old boy. These two royal children, used by others and old before their time, would come to share a decade of life and young love.

In the tomb, on a wooden chest veneered in ivory, Ankhesenamun stands, a diminutive figure beneath a bower, holding bouquets of poppies and lotus in both hands. She holds the flowers out to her sovereign lord, Tutankhamun, her dark hair flowing down her left shoulder, her diaphanous gown revealing abdomen and thigh.

On the great golden throne-chair she applies perfumed ointment to her husband's shoulder as he waits to appear before his courtiers. Rays of the benevolent sun descend and end in human hands holding the *ankh,* hieroglyphic symbol of life, to the nostrils of Tutankhamun, that he might inhale its vitalizing fragrance.

On the sides of a golden shrine, Ankhesenamun sits on a soft hassock as her husband pours perfumed water into her hand, her right breast visible through her bodice. In another setting, a papyrus marsh, Tutankhamun sits on a folding stool among the bulrushes, his pet lion crouching beside him. The king takes aim with bow and arrow as wild ducks, flushed from a papyrus thicket, take wing. Before him sits the young queen, holding another arrow in her hand for the time when her husband might require it, pointing with her other hand to a nest of fledglings and bidding him spare the birds' mother.

Such a papyrus marsh is the setting of yet another love poem from ancient Egypt, verses that could have been uttered by a young prince named Tutankhamun before the flowers of the wreath had been picked, before the final door was sealed.

> Even when the birds rise
> Wave mass on wave mass in great flight
> I see nothing, I am blind
> Caught up as I am and carried away

Two hearts obedient in their beating
My life caught up with yours
Your beauty the binding.[13]

*   *   *   *

Far from Egypt near the Turkish village of Boghazköy
sprawl the ruins of Hattusas, capital of the ancient Hittite
empire. Once the Hittites were among the mightiest nations
on earth, a military superpower that vied with Egypt for
control of the Near East; today their name is obscure even
to the educated—a humbling commentary on the place pres-
ent-day nation-states may someday have in humankind's
cultural memory.

Excavated at the beginning of the twentieth century, the
royal palace at Hattusas has yielded over ten thousand inscribed tablets, the archives of the Hittite empire. Among
the annals are two texts that bear upon the story of Ankhesenamun.

In one, a Hittite king named Mursilis describes the reign
of his father Suppiluliumas, a monarch of the fourteenth
century B.C. and a contemporary of Tutankamun. Tutankhamun's royal title, Nebkheperura, appears here in its Hittite
spelling, *Bibhururiyas* (*Nibhururiyas* in a more accurate parallel
text).

> Because . . . their lord Bibhururiyas [Tutankhamun] had
> just died, the Egyptian queen [Ankhesenamun] who had
> become a widow, sent an envoy to my father and wrote
> him as follows: "My husband died and I have no son.
> People say that you have many sons. If you were to send
> me one of your sons, he might become my husband. I am
> loathe to take a servant of mine and make him my hus-
> band."

> When my father heard that, he called the great into coun-
> cil (saying): "Since of old such a thing has never happened
> before me." He proceeded to dispatch Hattu-zitis, the
> chamberlain, (saying): "Go! Bring you reliable informa-

tion back to me. They may try to deceive me: As to whether they have a prince bring reliable information back to me!" . . . The Egyptian queen answered my father in a letter as follows: "Why do you say: 'They may try to deceive me?' If I had a son, would I write to a foreign country in a manner which is humiliating to myself and my country? You do not trust me and tell me even such a thing. He who was my husband died and I have no sons. Shall I perhaps take one of my servants and make him my husband? I have not written to any other country; I have only written to you. People say that you have many sons. Give me one of your sons and he is my husband and king in the land of Egypt."

Mursilis concludes:

Because my father was generous, he complied with the lady's wishes and decided for (sending) the son.[14]

For once Ankhesenamun had taken her destiny (and that of her nation) into her own hands, boldly offering kingship to a son of an enemy emperor and proposing a historic wedding of imperialistic rivals. She may well have feared that not to do so would mean being forced to marry someone else, perhaps someone she detested—for what he was or what he stood for. Instead, she decided to act, before the seventy days of mourning were ended and Tutankhamun's body was placed in its tomb.

Yet others, more powerful and even more devious, had learned of the secret message and decided to intervene. As Mursilis records in a later entry: "When my father gave them one of his sons, they killed him as they led him there."[15]

After this, little is heard of Ankhesenamun. An aged courtier named Eye becomes the next pharaoh; Ankhesenamun, his consort. Two years later, the powerful commander-in-chief of the army, Haremhab, takes the throne. Ankhesenamun is no longer mentioned in Egypt's (or anyone's) annals. Her tomb has never been found.

5

Ghost Towns of the Indus Valley

Toys in the Dust

HUMMING LOW through the rails, the train told the children it was coming. Urging one another on, they stepped up to the tracks that gleamed bright and hot in the Pakistani sun. In turn, each child knelt down, bending his ear to the rail to catch the song of the train. Louder and louder it grew until one of the children, looking down the tracks to Lahore, saw the first signs of smoke. Backing away as though in reverence at the coming of an elder, they sat down and peered in the direction of the smoke. Soon their ears picked up a faint shriek in the distance, a shriek that grew and grew, louder and more insistent, as the dark form of a machine rose on the horizon. Soon it was upon them in all its black, cindery, puffing majesty, screaming and clattering and then just as suddenly past, hurtling down the tracks with its obedient cars to the opposite horizon. Only its humming remained behind, reverberating in the iron rails and wooden ties and the bed of bricks beneath.

*   *   *   *

The construction of the East Indian Railway in 1856 had posed a special problem to the British: the soft, alluvial soil of the Indus Valley served as a poor foundation for heavy

Portrait of a god or priest-king from Mohenjo-daro.

ties and rails. Searching for a solution, engineer William Brunton discovered a ruined town southwest of Lahore, a town with buildings made of oven-baked brick. The town, known as Harappa, was dismantled, and its bricks carted by the millions to the work site where they were used to lay the railway bed.

In demolishing Harappa, the British were unknowingly demolishing history. Later archaeological research revealed that Harappa was once an important center of a vast and powerful ancient civilization that flourished in the latter half of the third millennium B.C., contemporary with Egypt's age of pyramids and Ur's third dynasty.

Along with its sister-city of Mohenjo-daro, three hundred fifty miles to the southwest, Harappa constituted the world's oldest example of urban planning. Each city was laid out on a grid-pattern with 30-foot-wide streets intersecting at right angles to form blocks. For privacy, house walls that faced the street had no windows; instead, homes had inner courtyards opening onto quiet residential lanes that led from the main thoroughfares. Above the residential portion of each city stood a strongly fortified citadel.

Extraordinary care was expended in providing for sanitation and hygiene. Families could empty their trash into chutes that poured into street-side rubbish bins made of brick. Every home also had a drain that led into a sewer system located beneath the city streets. The sewers, made of brick, were equipped with special pits to trap heavier waste and with manholes for inspection and servicing. Fresh water for drinking and sanitation was provided by a series of public and private wells. At Mohenjo-daro a public bathhouse, perhaps intended for ritual bathing, featured a 20- by 40-foot pool, waterproofed in asphalt, with an adjoining series of private rooms.

Altogether, the design of the Indus Valley cities—far in advance of Egypt and Sumeria—may be said to "reflect decent standards of living coupled with an obviously zealous municipal supervision."[16] In the uniform bricks and regimented blocks we sense a strong and central government. This impression is reinforced by one of the few stone sculptures of this culture to survive: the portrait of a priest-king or god from Mohenjo-daro. His darkly narrowed eyes, his sharply trimmed beard, and his emotionless lips convey a manner both obdurate and austere.

Another statue, a small figurine in bronze, seems almost to mock his air of aloofness. She may have been a dancing girl. "Naked but for a necklace and a series of bangles almost covering one arm, her hair dressed in a complicated coiffure, standing in a provocative posture, with one arm on her hip and one lanky leg half bent, this young woman has an air of lively pertness, quite unlike anything in the work of other ancient civilizations."[17]

*　　*　　*　　*

As far back as Brunton's demolition of Harappa, the attention of archaeologists had been drawn to a number of carved stone cubes found in the ruins. The lustrous white cubes measured about one inch on each side. On their backs, bosses had been fashioned and drilled so the stones could be hung from necklaces. Sculpted on their faces in intaglio with remarkable and sophisticated artistry were animals that once populated ancient Pakistan: elephant and tiger, crocodile and antelope, rhino and humpbacked ox, and—most common of all—a mythical, unicornlike bull.

. Also carved on the cubes were pictographs. Their total number—about 400—showed they were not the simple signs of an alphabet. Because an average of six were carved on each cube, they could have spelled out the name or title of the wearer, who would have used the seal as a signet-ring, pressing it into clay. Different from any known writing system, the Indus Valley script has so far defied all but the most tentative attempts at decipherment.

Less mysterious than the seal stones but no less fascinating are the terracotta toys that have been dug up at Indus Valley sites. Their variety and abundance recall how many children once played in the now faceless and silent streets.

There are marbles of agate and jasper, and hollow clay balls filled with hard pellets that rattled when rolled. There are also whistles in the shape of birds, each with a hole to blow in, set behind the tail. Miniature birds abound too, some in clay cages, some with beaks open in song.

Most ingenious are the animals that move. Some swivel their heads on pivots. An ox nods its head up and down, worked from behind by a straw that passed through its hump. And a clever monkey climbs down a string; passing through a bent channel in the monkey's fists, the string—when pulled taut—stopped the monkey's descent. The most common toy found was a two-wheeled clay cart drawn by oxen. In some, a driver still sits in his seat, whip in hand. "Playing house" was done in ancient India too: Miniature pans, shaped simply out of clay by the children themselves, still bear their little fingerprints.

*　　*　　*　　*

Why the cities died, no one knows. By 2000 B.C. Harappa and Mohenjo-daro were abandoned and soon became ghost towns, though elsewhere the culture of the Indus Valley survived. Some claim resources were used wastefully through overcultivation, overgrazing, and deforestation, until the environment could no longer support the large populations of the cities. Others theorize a sudden rise in the coastline, backing up the waters of the Indus and flooding the fields.

Skeletons, found in the streets and houses of Mohenjo-daro, have been taken as evidence of invasion, but there are no widespread signs of destruction, no charred remains, in the city. The skeletons, in fact, only about thirty in number, all come from the lower town rather than the citadel, the most logical target of attack. It is not even clear that the bodies all belong to the last phase of the city's history. At Harappa, moreover, no such scattered bodies have been found. It is probable that those who died at Mohenjo-daro died in a city already deserted.

Later in the second millennium B.C. warriors swept down over Pakistan and India, warriors who called themselves *aryas*, "the noble ones." The might of the Aryans thundered in the hooves of horses and the rush of chariots, weapons unknown in the land until then. With them the Aryan warriors brought a new language, Sanskrit, and composed hymns to celebrate their triumphs and their gods.

By the middle of the nineteenth century another conqueror, the British, governed the Indian subcontinent. The English engineers who laid the rail line from Karachi to Lahore did so across a land ignorant of its urban past. Train after train rumbled down tracks laid on ancient brick, brick that reverberated with the rhythmic song of iron and echoed with the sound of children playing on vanished streets.

6

The Legend of the Minotaur

The Dark Labyrinth

SECRET PASSIONS BEGIN in the darkness, and in the dark are hidden. In the darkness they hid the child—the strange, misshapen child born to the queen, boy-child with human body and horned head, child born of insatiable lust that drove the queen, cow-costumed, to mate with a bull.

Her husband, King Minos of Crete, could not bear to destroy his wife's offspring. He bade the chief craftsman of the palace, Daedalus, to design for it a home from which it could never escape. So Daedalus fashioned in the depth of the palace a maze from which exit was impossible. The maze they called the *Labyrinth;* the creature, the *Minotaur*—half man, half bull. There in the darkness of the Labyrinth it lived out its life.

Now Queen Pasiphaë had borne to Minos two daughters and a son. In later years the son was killed while on a mission to Athens. Enraged at his death, Minos pronounced judgment upon Athens: Every year seven young men and seven young women must be sent as human sacrifices to expiate the death of the Cretan prince. Led to the mouth of the Labyrinth, the victims would be forced to enter until, losing their way, they were inexorably led to its center where the deadly Minotaur waited.

For years the tradition of human sacrifice continued until

Portrait of a young Minoan woman, *La Parisienne.*

an Athenian prince named Theseus determined to end it once and for all. Begging his father, King Aegeus, to let him join the next company of victims, Theseus vowed to kill the beast. He would sail, he said, under black sails, but if victorious would change the sails to white on his homeward voyage as a sign of triumph.

Once in Crete the Athenian youths were brought to the royal palace at Knossos. There in the throne room sat Minos, and beside him his lovely daughter Ariadne. As soon as her eyes beheld the handsome, bronze-skinned prince she fell in love with him. How could she save him, she wondered.

For help she turned to Daedalus, the Labyrinth's designer. "Give the young man some thread," he advised her, "and have him let it out a little at a time as he moves through the Labyrinth. If he is hero enough to slay the monster, he can find his way back to safety by following the thread."

Ariadne did as she was told. Theseus was able to kill the Minotaur and, by following the thread, escaped the Labyrinth. Together Ariadne and Theseus sailed for Greece, stopping at an island way station when night fell.

But when Ariadne awoke the next morning, she found herself alone, deserted by the Greek stranger she had loved. Regarding her as expendable, Theseus had set sail for home by himself. But in his exhilaration at having slain the monster, he had forgotten to change the color of his sails from black to white. His father, standing on the Acropolis and scanning the horizon, saw the ship approaching and, to his horror, saw the black sails. Believing his son dead, King Aegeus hurled himself into the sea, by his death bestowing upon the sea the name *Aegean*.

Meanwhile, Minos discovered what had happened at the Labyrinth. Believing his architect responsible, Minos put Daedalus and Daedalus's son Icarus under house arrest. But using his ingenuity Daedalus devised a means of escape. He fashioned wings out of wax and feathers, one pair for himself and another for his son.

"Don't fly too high," warned Daedalus, "or the sun's rays will melt the wax!" Soon they were airborne, but Icarus, forgetting his father's admonition in the excitement of flight, climbed higher and higher, ever closer to the sun. At last his wings melted in the heat as his father had warned, and Icarus plummeted into the sea to his death. Grief stricken, Daedalus flew on until he reached Sicily, where Minos pursued him and eventually died.

Thus concludes the story of the Minotaur and the Labyrinth, one of the most famous chapters in Greek mythology. Later, Greek poets and historians would speak of King Minos and his vast power, but by the Classical period the civilization over which Minos ruled had sunk into the mist of legend.

*   *   *   *

In 1899 an Englishman named Arthur Evans stood on a large mound located near the north coast of Crete. He had come seeking the source of small semiprecious stones that had turned up on the Greek antiquities market, stones curiously engraved with human figures and mythic beasts and inscribed with symbols of a strange hieroglyphic script. The trail of stones had led Evans to the mound, a site identified by tradition as Knossos, the legendary seat of King Minos's power. Only recently, large ceramic jars had been dug out of the ancient rubble.

The excavations Evans was to begin would reveal the ruins of a vast palace that had once risen by grand staircases to a height of three or more stories and had contained over a thousand rooms. The interior had been equipped with running water and illuminated by architectural innovations called light-wells, vertical shafts that passed down from the roof through successive floors, allowing natural sunlight to be diffused into different levels of the palace. The walls of the rooms and halls were adorned with rich frescoes of playful dolphins and elegant processions of slim-waisted young men and women with long tresses of dark hair. The free-flowing hair of the women, their large eyes and ruby-red lips, and their air of insouciance reminded one French observer of the young women in his own turn-of-the-century Paris, and soon the most beautiful one of all was dubbed *La Parisienne*.

On one wall a great fresco showed male and female acrobats leaping over the horns of a charging bull, an event that may have been enacted in the great open courtyard found by Evans at the heart of the palace. Here too, perhaps, the young men and women had danced, as Homer in the *Iliad* recalls:

> Also did the glorious lame god devise a dancing-place like unto that which once in wide Knossos Daedalus wrought for Ariadne of the lovely tresses. There were youths dancing and maidens of costly wooing, their hands upon one another's wrists. Fine linen the maidens had on, and the youths well-woven doublets faintly glistening with oil. Fair wreaths had the maidens, and the youths daggers of gold hanging from silver baldrics. And now would they run round with deft feet exceeding lightly, as when a potter sitting by his wheel that fitteth between his hands maketh trial of it whether it run; and now anon they would run in lines to meet each other. And a great company stood round the lovely dance in joy; and among them a divine minstrel was making music on his lyre, and through the midst of them, leading the measure, two tumblers whirled.[18]

Inside the palace Evans found magnificent vases. On each was a painted octopus, its swirling tentacles and bulbous head filling out the bulging contours of each vase. In the basement, corridors were filled with huge ceramic jars. In the floors of the corridors were secret compartments that once held tribute. Even the inventory records, inscribed on clay tablets, survived. In a subterranean sanctuary Evans came upon two faience statuettes of a bare-breasted goddess. One statuette showed her holding a serpent in each hand; in the other the snakes curled their way up her arms. In another room of the palace Evans found a throne carved out of stone. Flanked by stone benches for counselors, the throne stood against a wall emblazoned with twin griffins. Evans had found the oldest surviving throne in European history, a throne more than three thousand years old.

The discoveries of Arthur Evans at Knossos revealed the existence of a lost Mediterranean civilization, a Shangri-la of the ancient Aegean, whose splendor and brilliance could now illuminate the legends that had for so long been associated with the island of Crete.

Again and again the image of a mighty bull appears in the art of the palace; even the stone altars of the palace are surmounted by bull's horns. Could the origin of the Minotaur lie in the sacred bull? Like the victims from Athens who had confronted the Minotaur, here on Crete young men and women had engaged in a potentially deadly encounter with a bull, defying death by leaping over its horns. If ritual sacrifices had been carried out by a priest wearing the mask of a bull, his terrifying appearance might well have inspired the image of a deadly creature half man, half beast.

The palace itself might have generated the notion of a labyrinth, for its basement was replete with myriad chambers and dark passageways. Even the name *labyrinth* recalls the palace, since it is derived from an ancient suffix that meant "place of" and a Minoan root, *labrys,* that meant "double ax." The sacrificial double ax, carved on walls and wrought in gold, was an ever-present symbol of Minoan civilization. Thus the Labyrinth was "the place of the double ax," a descriptive term for the palace itself.

The grandeur of Minoan civilization testifies to the existence of a king like Minos, whose achievement in building the world's first maritime empire was later remembered by Greek historians. The architectural and engineering wonders of the palace suggest the inventive genius of a Daedalus, a Cretan Leonardo da Vinci. Even the prototypes for his wings can be seen worn by figures on palace frescoes. As for Ariadne, her resourcefulness and initiative reflect the animated character of the young women who populate so much of Minoan art and who seem to have played such a central role in Minoan society. In the sensuous beauty of *La Parisienne* we may also catch intimations of Ariadne's own charm.

*   *   *   *

Seen in a different light, the discoveries at Knossos may serve as the background for yet another myth, the legend of the lost kingdom of Atlantis. First recorded in the writings of the Greek philosopher Plato,[19] the myth tells of a mighty island-based empire that once threatened Greece, especially Athens. The people of Atlantis possessed a knowledge of writing and metallurgy, and their religion included the hunting of wild bulls. Despite its vast power, the entire civilization disappeared suddenly, sinking beneath the sea in a single day and night.

The historical reality of Atlantis has long been doubted by historians. In his account, Plato reports that the story of Atlantis was first told by Egyptian wise men to Solon, an Athenian statesman and traveler of the early sixth century B.C. According to the Egyptians, Atlantis had disappeared nine thousand years before Solon's time, or sometime around 9550 B.C. Because it was not until approximately 3000 B.C. that the first civilizations of the world emerged, modern historians have regarded the existence of an advanced civilization thousands of years earlier as a virtual impossibility. Furthermore, oceanographers report that there is no submerged body of land in the Atlantic that could qualify as the last vestige of a sunken kingdom.

The Egyptian number system, however, may offer an important clue to the possible existence and location of Atlantis. The ancient Egyptian numbers for *hundred* and *thousand* sound enough alike to confuse someone barely familiar with that language. If Solon thought the Egyptians had said nine *thousand,* but in fact they had said nine *hundred,* the date for Atlantis's disappearance would change from 9550 B.C. (9000 + 550) to 1450 B.C. (900 + 550), a date well within the range of Minoan civilization's life span.

Recent archaeological discoveries have provided further clues in the search for Atlantis. The island of Santorini, known in ancient times as Thera, is the southernmost of the Aegean islands known as the Cyclades. Like other Aegean isles, Thera is the top of an underwater mountain, but unlike the others the mountain is volcanic. In approximately 1450 B.C. a cataclysmic eruption occurred there, the largest volcanic eruption known to have taken place on this planet. The entire center of the island was blown apart, leaving what may well be the world's largest volcanic crater—almost forty miles wide. The remnant edges of the island were to hang thereafter as sheer cliffs poised above waves nine hundred feet below.

The might of the volcanic explosion would have been equivalent to the force of a four-hundred-megaton nuclear bomb. From the center of the explosion, tidal waves three hundred feet high would have hurtled outward at a speed of two hundred miles per hour. The north shore of Crete, lying about seventy miles south of Thera, would have been struck in twenty minutes. Poisonous gas would also have been emitted from the volcano as well as hundreds of tons of ash, thrown into the sky in such quantity that day would have become night. This ash can still be detected in deep-sea cores extracted from the floor of the Mediterranean.

Excavations on Thera by the late Spyridon Marinatos have revealed the remains of a Minoan settlement buried at the island's edge under deep layers of ash and pumice. From the ruins of this Minoan "Pompeii" have emerged the remains of private homes, including a ceramic bathtub decorated with painted dolphins, graceful vases ornamented with plant and bird motifs, and frescoes, astonishing for their scope and vibrant colors. In these frescoes blue monkeys frolic in a red and yellow jungle, lovebirds flutter their wings over swaying lilies, two boys bravely box, a proud fisherman holds his catch, and an elaborate flotilla of Minoan ships sails into a Cretan harbor. The absence of widespread skeletal remains suggests that volcanic tremors gave the populace enough warning to permit escape.

The time of the eruption comes close to two changes in the archaeological record of the Aegean. Before 1450 B.C., the pottery found on Aegean islands is of Minoan manufacture (evidence of the commercial power of Crete); later, however, the pottery is of mainland manufacture (evidence that the control of trade had shifted from Minoan to Greek hands). Before 1450 B.C., inventory records in the palace of Knossos were kept in a script called *Linear A*; after 1450 B.C., bookkeeping records were kept in a different script called *Linear B*. Thanks to a decipherment by amateur cryptographer Michael Ventris and his partner, Classical philologist John Chadwick, we know that the Linear B inscriptions are in Greek. To date, the Linear A texts have not been fully deciphered, but they are definitely written in a non-Greek language. The widespread presence of Greek-made pottery in the Aegean and the use of Greek for bookkeeping records at Knossos points to a Greek takeover of commerce in the Aegean, and, very likely, a Greek political and military takeover at Knossos.

The eruption on Thera may well have set the stage for these changes. Unlike the stoutly fortified palaces of the Bronze Age Greeks, the palaces of the Minoans are essentially unfortified, even though some could easily be attacked from the sea. It is likely, however, that they were protected by another line of defense, one formed by the ships of the Minoan merchant marine that would normally have controlled the sea-lanes of the Aegean.

If, however, a cataclysmic explosion had generated massive tidal waves, the bulk of such a fleet could have been sunk. The covetous Greeks to the north, always adventurous and aggressive, could have seized the opportunity and invaded Crete, establishing their base of operations at Knossos, installing their own bookkeepers, and taking over trade in the Aegean. The burnt remains of the palace may testify to a subsequent counterrevolution led by vengeful Minoans who sought to drive out their Greek overlords by force.

In later days such turns of history could have been transformed into legend: a Greek Theseus would come to stand triumphant over the fallen Minotaur of Crete, and an empire overwhelmed by the sea would live on in the imagination as the lost kingdom of Atlantis.

Was there then no real Ariadne, no Theseus, no real romance? Or did a bronze-skinned stranger stand one day in the crowd at Knossos as the sacred bull rushed from its chute? Did a princess turn away from the acrobats to gaze at him? And did the fate of empires shudder as he returned her glance and smiled, thinking all the while of profit and loss?

7

The Ruins of Troy

Where Heroes Walked

DEEP WITHIN THE PALACE at the dark meeting place of torch-lit corridors was the door to the great hall. Into the stone-columned sanctuary no sounds of the battlefield could enter—no clank and thud of sword and shield, no brazen shout of enemy against foe. Here only the crackling of wood on the blazing hearth could be heard and the soothing sound of the woman singing, her face colored golden by the fire's light. Her arms moved back and forth as she plied the great loom, agile hands weaving the story of men battling and dying, of men battling and dying for her. From her fingers the wool of bright skeins took on human form, rising as proud warriors on the field of battle. There stood her vengeful husband Menelaus, Sparta's king; against him strode Paris, her handsome lover, whose passion first bore her to Troy's windy heights. Along the shore were arrayed the thousand ships that had sailed warrior-laden from Greece to win her back; ahead rose the battlements of Troy, rimmed with defenders, brave Hector among them. In the Greek camp stood Agamemnon, lord of golden Mycenae and commander-in-chief; crafty Ulysses from far-off Ithaca; and savage, man-slaying Achilles. If her beauty could bring on deadly war, her skill could make of war a work of art. Alone

Golden funeral mask from the grave circle at Mycenae.

in the great hall, Helen hummed a lullaby to the beauty of her design.

*　　*　　*　　*

Legend tells that the origin of the Trojan War was the wedding of two worlds that could only perilously be joined: the world of human beings and the world of the gods. Decades before the war a divine sea nymph named Thetis had fallen in love with a mortal named Peleus. Wishing strife to be absent from their marriage, the lovers deliberately excluded the goddess of discord from those invited to their wedding. Nevertheless she came, true to her name, bringing to the wedding feast a golden apple inscribed with the words "To the fairest." Cunningly, she set it on the banquet table before three goddesses, knowing that out of vanity each would claim it as her own. The three deities were Hera, queen of the Greek gods; Athena, goddess of wisdom; and Aphrodite, goddess of love. After squabbling over the apple, the goddesses brought their suit before Zeus, king of the gods, who in turn sent them to a youth of royal blood named Paris, then shepherding a flock near Troy. Appearing before Paris, each beauty contestant offered him a bribe to win the prize. Hera promised him sovereign power; Athena, deep wisdom; Aphrodite, the love of the most beautiful woman on earth. It was Aphrodite's offer that most appealed to the amorous young Paris and incurred for him (and his Trojan race) the eternal enmity of Athena and Hera.

Years later, Aphrodite fulfilled her pledge. When Paris was visiting the Greek city of Sparta, he met its queen, the beautiful Helen. Under Aphrodite's sway, Helen fell in love with the handsome Paris and decided to sail with her lover to Troy, forsaking her husband Menelaus.

When King Menelaus found Helen and Paris gone, he turned to his brother for aid. Menelaus's brother, Agamemnon, was the king of Mycenae, the most powerful fortress-city in all of Greece. Reminding his vassals of their feudal obligations to him, Agamemnon called upon all the kings and princes of the land to rally to the defense of his brother's honor. Thus the combined heroic might of Greece was hurled against the city of Troy.

Motives less than romantic may have also set the war in motion. In an acquisitive culture, stealing Helen constituted an affront to her husband's dignity. In addition, Troy's strategic location on the Turkish coast near the strait connecting the Black Sea with the Mediterranean gave it the power to levy taxes on Greek merchant ships. The destruction of the city and the plundering of its riches would have added immeasurably to the coffers of the Greek warlords. Thus Helen's abduction may have been the convenient pretext for an invasion already planned.

Troy was no easy target, though. Stoutly fortified and reinforced by its allies from the Turkish interior, embattled Troy struggled on against siege for ten years.

Killed in battle were some of the greatest fighters on each side, including Achilles, acknowledged as the fiercest and most feared warrior to come to Troy. Achilles was the only child of Peleus and Thetis, whose perilous marriage had led to the war. According to legend, the young Achilles had been given a choice by the Fates: to live a long life of obscurity or to live a life that was glorious but short. Achilles chose to be remembered forever, driven by a compulsive need for fame and honor. Yet in this quest Achilles would bring about the tragic death of his closest friend, Patroclus. Finally, Achilles himself would fall, struck by an arrow shot by Paris. Ironically, the arrow would strike the one part of Achilles's body that was vulnerable, his heel. For that is where his goddess mother had held him when she baptized him in the sacred river Styx.

In the end Troy fell not to open attack but to deception. In the tenth year of the war the Greek army suddenly broke camp and sailed for home. On the deserted beach they left behind a gigantic horse fashioned out of wood. Believing the wooden horse to be a good-luck charm, the Trojans dragged it into the heart of their citadel and began their victory celebration.

In the dead of the night, with the Trojans fast asleep, a concealed door opened in the belly of the wooden horse, a rope ladder dropped out, and a cluster of Greek commandos who had been hiding inside descended. They opened the city gates and signaled by torchlight to the rest of the army, lying in wait in their ships behind an offshore island. Soon all Troy was ablaze with fire, and the cries of the wounded and dying rang out.

With Troy in ashes, the Greeks sailed for home, their ships loaded with treasure. Helen was reunited with Menelaus. Though she would return with him to live out her days in Sparta, she would be known forever as Helen "of Troy." King Agamemnon returned to golden Mycenae, only to be murdered by his wife and her lover. As for Ulysses, ten more years of adventures on the sea awaited him before he would see his beloved Ithaca again and be reunited with his family.

The tales of Troy came to be enshrined in two ancient Greek epics, Homer's *Iliad* and *Odyssey,* the oldest surviving works of Western literature and the oldest surviving poems in any European language. The *Iliad* tells of Achilles and the final year of the war; the *Odyssey* tells of Ulysses and his homeward voyage. The two poems were revered by the Classical Greeks as scripture, for they embodied exemplars of human courage and nobility. Roman Vergil would imitate them in his *Aeneid.* The poems would also have profound influence upon later ages of Western culture, where for so long a knowledge of Homer was rightly looked upon as a necessary ingredient of education.

Yet are these works based upon real history, or are they rather episodes from mythology? Are they fact or fiction? Did a Helen or a Paris, an Achilles or a Ulysses, ever really live? Was there ever a place called Troy?

*   *   *   *

To most nineteenth-century university professors of history the tales of Homer belonged to the world of legend. But for a young boy growing up in a small nineteenth-century German village the vivid tales of ancient cities and brave heroes, recounted in majestic verse, could only be true. Though only eight years old, as he later recalled, young Heinrich Schliemann vowed that some day he would find Troy. As he grew to manhood, he rose in station guided by a prodigious memory and stern self-discipline, eventually amassing a fortune as a merchant. Yet, according to his memoirs, he never surrendered his dream of finding Troy.

A reconnaissance Schliemann had made of the Turkish coast convinced him that the ruins of Troy lay at a mound called Hissarlik (Turkish for "fortress"). Here in Classical times had stood a city the Romans called Novum Ilium (New Troy). Surely, near the base of the mound, Schliemann thought, must lie the remains of the old Troy of Homeric saga. The mound was near the shore (where the Greeks could have beached their ships and encamped) and it overlooked a broad plain (where chariots could have raced and armies clashed). The size of the site reflected a once powerful city, and broken pottery found scattered on its surface confirmed that it had indeed been occupied. Few scholars agreed with Schliemann's identification; some proposed an alternate site, but none cared as Schliemann did to find the incontravertible proof. For Schliemann, finding Troy had become an obsession.

In 1871, after securing permission from the Turkish authorities to dig, Schliemann commenced excavation by cutting a trench through the mound to reach the very heart of the buried city. But after he had sliced through the mound, he realized he was excavating not one city but many, the ruins of multiple settlements from different time periods, superimposed one above the other, not unlike the layers of a lopsided seven-layer cake. Because each layer, or stratum, of ruins represented a different time period, Schliemann would have to distinguish the layers from one another, peeling them away one at a time and examining their contents. By trial and error coupled with alternating patience and frustration, Heinrich Schliemann developed the basic methods of stratigraphic excavation that archaeologists still use to this day. Although he had not anticipated it, Schliemann would become one of the founders of modern archaeology.

Beside him in his excavation of Troy was his bride Sophia, who shared his reverence for Homer. During the years they were to spend as coworkers at Troy, surely the most exciting single moment for the two was the first discovery of gold, a cache that Heinrich Schliemann would proudly call "the Treasure of Priam," after the name of Troy's legendary king.

In excavating this wall further and directly by the side of the palace of King Priam, I came upon a large copper article of the most remarkable form, which attracted my attention all the more as I thought I saw gold behind it. On the top of this copper article lay a stratum of red and calcined ruins, from 4¾ to 5¼ feet thick, as hard as stone, and above this again lay the above-mentioned wall of fortification (6 feet broad and 20 feet high) which was built of large stones and earth, and must have belonged to an early date after the destruction of Troy. In order to withdraw the Treasure from the greed of my workmen, and to save it for archaeology, I had to be most expeditious, and although it was not yet time for breakfast, I immediately had "païdos" [a rest period] called .... While the men were eating and resting, I cut out the Treasure with a large knife, which it was impossible to do without the very greatest exertion and the most fearful risk of my life, for the great fortification-wall, beneath which I had to dig, threatened every moment to fall down upon me. But the sight of so many objects, every one of which is of inestimable value to archaeology, made me foolhardy, and I never thought of any danger. It would, however, have been impossible for me to have removed the Treasure without the help of my dear wife, who stood by me ready to pack the things which I cut out in her shawl and to carry them away.

As I found all these articles together, forming a rectangular mass, or packed into one another, it seems to be certain that they were placed on the city wall in a wooden chest, ... such as those mentioned by Homer as being in the palace of King Priam. This appears to be the more certain, as close by the side of these articles I found a copper key above 4 inches long, the head of which (about 2 inches long and broad) greatly resembles a large safe-key of a bank.

It is probable that some member of the family of King Priam hurriedly packed the Treasure into the chest and carried it off without having time to pull out the key; that when he reached the wall, however, the hand of an enemy or the fire overtook him, and he was obliged to abandon the chest, which was immediately covered to a height of from 5 to 6 feet with the red ashes and stones of the adjoining royal palace.[20]

The treasure Schliemann had found included bronze tools, silver goblets and bowls, and golden pieces of jewelry, among them eighty-six hundred gold beads and two magnificent golden diadems (worn by a proud Sophia in a historic photograph). The treasure trove was one of sixteen that the Schliemanns would find in the ruins called Troy II, the second settlement on the site. It was this rich second city, also called "the Burnt City" from its charred remains, that Schliemann identified as the Troy captured by the Greeks and set to the torch.

Interrupting his work at Troy, Heinrich Schliemann traveled to Greece in search of golden Mycenae, the capital city of Agamemnon, the leader of the Greek war against Troy. Excavating at a ruined citadel above the Greek village that still bore Mycenae's name, Schliemann uncovered a massive stone gateway surmounted by a triangular slab of stone carved with the heraldic symbol of the Mycenaean royal family: twin lions, symbols of prowess, their front paws resting on a columned altar—the oldest surviving work of monumental sculpture in the history of European art.

Excavating inside the gateway, Schliemann came upon a cemetery containing the graves of Mycenae's royalty. Stacked one above the other in shafts, their faces covered with masks of beaten gold, were the bones of Mycenae's kings. Beside them were golden wine cups for the heroic banquets of the afterlife when they would boast to their ghostly comrades of their brave deeds; and also close by, the instruments of their valor, bronze swords overlaid in yellow and white gold with scenes of hunting and war. Defying the dictum that "you can't take it with you," one king had even been buried with a set of solid gold balance scales to help him count and recount his wealth in the kingdom of Hades.

Queens were there too, their graves resplendent with golden ornaments, including a set of gold-foil butterflies to adorn the hair. Altogether Schliemann found over thirty-three pounds of solid gold in the shaft graves. And above the grave circle were stairs that led to the halls and rooms of a once mighty palace.

As Heinrich Schliemann lifted the golden mask of one of the buried kings, he beheld the royal face still intact. Suddenly, the distance between himself and the world of Homer's heroes melted away.

> The round face, with all its flesh, had been wonderfully preserved under its ponderous golden mask; there was no vestige of hair, but both eyes were perfectly visible, also the mouth, which, owing to the enormous weight that had pressed upon it, was wide open, and showed thirty-two beautiful teeth.[21]

Schliemann could well believe he was gazing upon the face of Agamemnon.

Discrepancies in date between his discoveries at Mycenae and at Troy would later cause Schliemann to question his identification of Troy II as Homer's Troy. The heroic age of Mycenae to which the warriors belonged, the fifteenth century B.C., would have been contemporary not with Troy II but with a later period in Troy's history, perhaps the mighty Troy VI, whose remains like those of Troy II bore evidence of destruction. To his dying day, Schliemann struggled with the question of which Troy was the Troy whose glory Homer had sung. Ironically, the correct layer was beneath his feet all the time. Today, archaeologists following in Schliemann's footsteps have identified Troy VIIa (the first

part of the seventh layer) as the remains of the city that fell
to the Greeks.

Troy VIIa existed at the same time as the fortress cities of
mainland Greece from which the invasion would have come.
Its ruins testify to its violent, fiery end. Skeletons of men
who died defending the city have been found in its streets.
Crowded inside the city walls are the remains of simple huts
built by those who moved into the citadel for safety when
war threatened. Dug into the floors of the huts are cisterns
meant to hold emergency supplies of food and drink during
siege. The city's fall can now be dated to about 1260 B.C.
Thus the famous "treasure of Priam" and "mask of Agamemnon" really belong to an earlier time, to the ancestors
of those who fought at Troy.

If one were to search the ruins of Troy VIIa for gold, one
would find only disappointment. The city was thoroughly
and meticulously sacked. (No wonder it did not catch
Schliemann's eye.) No jewelry remains, only the empty
molds into which the precious metal was once poured. A
corroding bronze arrow-point of Greek design recalls the
conquerors. Gone are Achilles and Hector, Paris and Helen.
Instead, scattered in the dust are worthless spindle whorls,
small flywheels of baked clay once fitted to spindles by
Trojan women as they spun their yarn. Perhaps one had
even been held by Helen as she sat before her loom, weaving
a tale of beauty and death.

*   *   *   *

A thousand years or more after the Trojan War, a Greek
writer named Lucian wondered why so many men had given
up their lives in Helen's name. In a satiric dialogue,[22] he
made a dead philosopher named Menippus (who had newly
arrived in Hades) ask the god Hermes for a guided tour. As
Hermes pointed out the most distinguished residents of
Hades, Menippus stood confused. "All I see are bones and
naked skulls," he said, "and they all look alike."

"And yet," answered Hermes, "those are what all the
poets admire, the things you call bones and despise."

"Perhaps," agreed Menippus, "but point Helen out to me. I can't find her myself."

"This skull," said Hermes, "is Helen."

Menippus stood there amazed. "Was *this* the reason," he asked, "why a thousand ships were manned by men from all over Greece and Greek and Trojan armies died and cities were laid waste?"

"Yes," Hermes said. "But you didn't see the woman when she was alive, or even *you* would have understood why 'for such a woman they suffered woe for so long.' Flowers, when they are dried out and faded, look ugly; but when they are in bloom and have color are beautiful indeed."

"Granted," said Menippus. "But didn't the Greeks know what a transient thing they were striving for, and how soon its bloom would fade?"

*   *   *   *

In the dust of Troy there is no testament to the brave or even a memorial to the reason for their dying. But in the spring, in the broad plain beneath the ruins of the citadel, wildflowers red as blood wave in the wind.

8

Underwater Archaeology in the Mediterranean

Greek Gods from the Sea

SILENTLY, SPEAR GUN IN HAND, he glided through the green-blue water in search of squid. Suddenly he saw it ahead of him—a hand and arm reaching out of the sand. He swam toward it quickly, diving and rapidly scooping the sand away. However, the arm was not flesh and blood but bronze, the green, corroded bronze of an ancient statue lost beneath the sea. As the scuba diver scanned the sea floor in excitement, he saw in the distance a second figure coming to life, a bronze knee rising up out of the sand.

The swimmer was an Italian chemist on holiday, Stefano Mariottini. Staying at the coastal resort town of Riace Marina, near the tip of the Italian boot, he had decided to spend the last morning of his vacation spearfishing in shallow water about a thousand feet from the beach. Now back on shore, Mariottini placed a call to the regional superintendent for archaeology, Dr. Giuseppe Foti, who summoned a police diving team to help raise the statues.

Hauled out of the water, the two statues stood larger than life, almost seven feet tall and weighing nearly a thousand pounds apiece. Both were bearded warriors: The handles of their shields still clung to their left forearms; their right hands were still open as though holding spears. One warrior

Bronze statue of a Greek hero from the waters of Riace Marina.

wore a helmet; the other, a fillet, or ribbon of honor, across his forehead. Though warriors, they stood naked to reveal through their smooth-muscled power and poised beauty the heroic magnificence of the human physique. Each exuded a confident pride in man and human potential, a spirit which, along with their naturalistic style, pointed to their origin in the second half of the fifth century B.C., the days of Greece's Golden Age.

Just as the salt-encrusted hero Ulysses had needed a bath after coming ashore, shipwrecked and naked, on the magical island of Phaeacia, so these two ancient Greek warriors needed to be cleansed before meeting the public. Their bath was to take much longer than Ulysses's and was to be far more elaborate. Three years were spent in the laboratory of the nearby National Museum of Reggio Calabria, where superficial dirt was removed. Then the warriors were transported to Florence's Archaeological Museum which, since the devastating flood of 1966, had become a world center for developing and applying scientific techniques to clean and restore damaged works of art. Over the course of the next five years their skin was cleansed of encrustations and corrosion with special scalpels, tiny compressed-air hammers, and ultrasonic equipment. Holes were cut into their feet to permit internal cleaning, while steel rods were inserted in their legs to add structural strength. At last, in 1980, eight years after their initial discovery, the two statues were put on public display in Florence.

The lengthy cleaning process had restored the warriors to nearly perfect condition. Their eyes still shone with inlaid ivory. Their eyelashes, lips, and nipples—originally applied in bright copper—gleamed against the dark contrast of their bronze bodies. The teeth of one warrior were still stunningly plated in glistening silver. Though only statues, the warriors radiated an awesome power. "It is so heroical," said a scholar of one warrior, "so full of itself, so mightily angry with its huge silver teeth—you could not live with it in your room. It emanates such a vivid presence that it is practically intolerable."[23] A reporter covering the exhibition was to speak of the statues as "presences of extraordinary power—so much so that they command, and even tyrannize, the visitors' attention. The crowds move as if magnetized by a supernatural force. Cries of admiration are continually heard, but they are mixed with expressions of awe and even of terror."[24]

* * * *

Where had these Greek warriors come from with their power to command and terrorize still intact after twenty-five centuries? And how had they come to rest on the floor of the Mediterranean Sea?

Art historians theorize that the statues were once part of the cargo of a ship from Greece bound for Italy. The ship would have sailed in the days when Rome was becoming master of the Mediterranean, when victorious generals and later emperors stripped Greek cities and sanctuaries of their treasures in order to beautify villas and glorify the city built on seven hills. Such a ship could have foundered in a storm at sea and gone down with its cargo. Or, seeking to lighten her load, the ship's captain may have ordered such heavy metal works jettisoned.

The Riace bronzes are not the only ancient Greek statues to have been lost in storms at sea and later recovered—as discoveries made in the 1920s reveal. Off the Greek coast near Marathon, site of a famous Greek victory, an almost life-size statue of an adolescent boy was found by fishermen. Like the statues from Riace, he was made of hollow bronze with his nipples inset in copper. His eyes were of white stone set with yellow glass irises rimmed in black. His right arm is upraised; his left hand, outstretched—as though he was picking fruit and placing it in a now-vanished bowl.

Near treacherous Cape Artemisium, in northern Greece, fishermen found a bronze boy jockey and the horse he rode. In the same general location divers also found the bronze body of a Greek god. He stands with legs spread out, arms extended and balanced, making ready to hurl a lost missile at an unseen enemy in the distance. From the open position of the fingers on his throwing hand, we can tell that he once held a spearlike weapon. Such a god was Poseidon, god of the sea, who used the trident as his weapon. The statue's superhuman height is 6'10"; the span of his arms almost the same at 6'11". His bearded face is devoid of all emotion; all instead is concentration. In its condensed strength and balanced pose, the statue of Poseidon from Cape Artemisium embodies the spiritual dynamism of the Greek Golden Age. With what justice the sea itself preserved this potent image of the god who once called it his domain!

But the sea has preserved the purity of Greek art as well. Original Greek statues survived Europe's Dark Ages only by a miracle: medieval Christians destroyed Greek art with such iconoclastic fury that we have not a single original statue that survives from the acknowledged hand of a master Greek sculptor. It is thanks to literary descriptions and the many copies made for the affluent and culture-hungry Roman market that we know what we do about these lost masterpieces and the artists who made them. But there is another reason that explains the loss of such statues. In a technologically dark age, bronze statues became a ready source of usable metal. Only rarely—by a violent act of nature (a storm at sea or an avalanche of stone)—were these ancient works of art protected from the willfulness of man. Though they are unsigned, these resurrected statues testify with a resonant authentic voice, as copies cannot, to the majesty and vision of Greek artisanship.

Yet there are dangers inherent in the attempt to harvest the sea of its ancient riches. Many ancient wrecks lie at depths that push compressed-air diving to its theoretical limit. Narcosis (a life-threatening dulling of judgment from the buildup of carbon dioxide in the bloodstream), air embolism (the bursting of the lungs through panic ascent), and the insidious "bends" (the bubbling up of nitrogen in the blood from rapid decompression, often leading to permanent paralysis and death) are the invisible companions of the diver. In addition, special handicaps exist when, rather than simply trying to salvage treasure from a wreck, a deliberate attempt is made to excavate a wreck site methodically, for it is no easy matter to adapt the techniques of surface excavation to a marine environment.

The beginnings of marine archaeology can be traced to 1900. Two Greek sponge-fishing boats, on their way home from working the North African coast, were forced by a storm to seek shelter at the Greek island of Antikythera. Not wanting to waste time as he waited for the winds to subside, the captain, Dimitrios Kondos, had his chief diver, Elias Stadiatis, descend in the hope of harvesting additional sponges. After a normal descent, Stadiatis suddenly bobbed up in the water gesticulating wildly. With his helmet off he told of seeing "horses and naked women." What he had in fact come upon was the sculptural cargo of an ancient wreck poised precariously at the edge of an undersea cliff. In a follow-up dive Kondos himself brought up an ancient bronze arm and later informed the Greek government of the discovery. With support vessels from the Greek navy, the exhausted sponge divers continued working the wreck two hundred feet beneath the sea as storm winds raged overhead.

The diving operation yielded the bronze head of a Hellenistic Greek philosopher, whose penetrating, truth-seeking gaze is alive today despite the passage of millennia. A tall and relaxed athlete in bronze was also recovered. From the open fingers of his extended right hand he seems to be softly pitching a ball to an invisible catcher. More humble objects were also found, like wine jars and pottery the style of which, along with the carbon dating of the ship's timbers, has placed the time of the wreck in the late days of the Roman republic.

The single most fascinating object proved to be a calcified lump of corroded bronze that was thought at first to be the fragment of some work of sculpture. As it dried in Athens' National Museum, it split open, revealing a curious multi-geared clockwork mechanism with dials marked off in degrees and inscribed in Greek with astronomical symbols. Examined many years later by English physicist and mathematician Derek de Solla Price, it was discovered to be a scientific instrument that could predict the rising and setting of major stars and constellations, the phases of the moon, and the movements of the planets. A testament to Greek scientific ingenuity, it is the most complex ancient scientific instrument we have and the oldest surviving computer in the world. It had last been set (from the frozen coordinates of its month and zodiac slip rings) in the year 80 B.C.

Since the discoveries at Antikythera, modern technology has come to the aid of marine archaeology. The invention in 1943 of the *s*elf-*c*ontained *u*nderwater *b*reathing *a*pparatus (scuba) has given divers new mobility, and, in more recent years, television has simplified the task of underwater reconnaissance. Forced-air "vacuum cleaner" tubes now aid in the rapid lifting of sand and small artifacts, and the recent development of color sonar offers the archaeologist the possibility of not only locating buried objects on the sea floor but also identifying their composition before diving.

Underwater archaeology demands a special breed of archaeologist: a scientist and humanist who is a diver as well. Yet the rewards are there for such a new breed, for the floor of the Mediterranean remains a vast and unexplored reservoir of ancient information and modern adventure. In its depths, bronze gods and heroes still sleep.

9

The Tombs of the Etruscans

The Mirrors of Time

IN THE EIGHTH CENTURY B.C., more than two thousand years before the birth of the Italian Renaissance, the first great civilization of Italy arose. Called Etruscan, it arose in the very same part of Italy—the land between the Arno and the Tiber called Tuscany—where the Renaissance was later born. And just as the artists of the Renaissance excelled in painting, so did their Etruscan forebears.

The painting of the Etruscans, the supreme testament to the creative energy of their culture, survives because of their religious beliefs. Like the Egyptians the Etruscans believed in the certainty of a vibrant life after death. Like the people of the Nile they believed that art, applied to the walls of a tomb, could help ensure for loved ones the continuation of the life they had known in this existence, that paintings on tomb walls could magically come to life. The Etruscans in fact invested so much energy in the making of tombs and tomb art that we know them best not through the ruins of the cities where they lived but from their cemeteries. The very survival of these "cities of the dead" has endowed Etruscan civilization with an immortality all its own.

The earthen mounds heaped on tombs (as at Cerveteri) announced the existence of buried treasure to Italian peasants long ago, and have resulted in centuries-long looting.

Etruscan husband and wife portrayed on a sarcophagus from Cerveteri.

Other tombs, quarried underground out of subsurface lime-stone (as at Tarquinia) remained secure, except for acciden-tal discovery. Hundreds upon hundreds of such tombs still lie buried. Using aerial photography, today's archaeologists try to detect any unevenness of ground or vegetation that may indicate the presence of underground structures; using potentiometers on the surface, they measure the resistance to the flow of electrical currents in the hope of detecting hollow chambers in the ground. Once a hole is bored into its ceiling, an entire tomb can be inspected and photo-graphed without excavation by means of a specially devel-oped periscope equipped with lights at one end and a camera mounted at the other.

Opening a tomb can endanger its art by subjecting deli-cate paintings to changing levels of temperature and humid-ity. Even in sealed tombs, water—seeping through the porous limestone walls—can eat away the skin of painted plaster. These dangers make urgent the task of photograph-ically recording Etruscan tombs and often have demanded the surgical removal of a painted surface to the protective environment of a museum.

In contrast to their dark setting, the tomb paintings of the Etruscans reveal a fervent love of life; in their portrayal of life's joys and nature's beauties the paintings constitute a defiance both of the death and of the very subterranean context in which they were created. In the frescoes nature plays a prominent role, for the banquets the dead enjoy are actually picnics held outdoors beneath the sun. Above the trees and flying across the sky we see birds of many colors, bright and airy symbols of freedom from earth's contain-ment.

It is an afterlife that is interpreted in sensuous terms with each of the five senses gratified: the sense of hearing by song-birds and the music of woodwind and lyre; of sight by the motion of birds and dancers; of taste by the flavor of food and drink conveyed by servants; of smell by wine's aroma and the scent of flowered garlands worn around the banqueters' necks; and of touch by the embrace of husband and wife. Eternal happiness is portrayed as man and woman in sensuous harmony with nature. Depicted many times in these scenes is the egg, held in the hand of a banqueter, a symbol (as at Easter) of resurrection.

Some paintings reveal the special interests of the deceased: wrestlers grappling in one tomb and fishermen in another bobbing up and down in a boat as a naked young man, pushed off a rock by a playful friend, dives into a sea of dolphins.

Etruscan painters worked swiftly, sketching and then applying mineral or vegetable pigments to the plastered walls while the walls were still wet. Though their palette was limited (black, white, red and pink, blue and green), their conceptions exude vitality. Moreover, the naturalistic style of many of the paintings reveals the Etruscans' love of contemporary Greek art.

The bodies of the dead were placed in sarcophagi, carved coffins of stone or baked clay fashioned to resemble the deceased reclining at the banquet. Some sarcophagi portray the married couple enjoying the afterlife together—she serving her husband food, he with goblet raised high—gentle archaic smiles upon their lips.

As the funeral procession descended the steep staircase to the crypt, long shadows thrown by the light of oil lamps must have danced on the frescoed walls. Lit by the flickering flames, images of painted dancers moved with graceful animation in time with silent rhythms. Warmed in the orange glow, pairs of painted banqueters, ruddy-complexioned men and fair-skinned wives, reclined on couches and embraced eternally.

The mourners, ascending the stairs and leaving the chamber behind, would have borne with them—from paintings that had come to life—memories of a radiant celebration amid the darkness.

*   *   *   *

Many objects have been discovered in Etruscan tombs, placed there for use by the deceased in the next life. Among these are vases, some locally made with shiny black finish, others imported from Greece with painted pictures on their surfaces, and golden jewelry characteristically ornamented with a profusion of tiny golden globules.

Among the buried objects one recurs with great frequency: the mirror, not made of reflective glass but of polished bronze formed in the shape of a disc and attached to a sculptured bronze handle. The mirror appears so frequently not only because it would serve the deceased's everyday needs in the afterlife but also because it symbolized the very essence of that afterlife—a reflection of the experiences the individual had known in his or her past existence. Who were these Etruscans who looked into the mirror of time?

According to the Greek historian Herodotus, who lived during the fifth century B.C., the Etruscans did not always live in Italy. Herodotus tells us that they originally came from a land known in ancient times as Lydia, located in central Turkey. Driven by famine from their homeland, half the Lydian population journeyed with their prince in search of a new country. Having sailed westward, they came upon Italy, where they settled and flourished.

Herodotus's belief that the Etruscans were immigrants is supported by many different types of evidence. Among ancient inscriptions that survive from Turkey are words and roots found also in Etruscan. They include the Etruscans own national name for themselves, *Rasena,* as well as the root *tarq* found in the city-name, *Tarquinia,* and in the title, *Tarquin,* a term for the Etruscan overlords who at one time ruled Rome. In addition, inscriptions in the Etruscan alphabetic script have been found on the Greek island of Lemnos just off the Turkish coast (and a possible stepping-stone to the west).

Etruscan origins in the East are also indicated by certain features of Etruscan culture that resemble similar features found among ancient cultures of the East Mediterranean world: a high level of metallurgical skill, the use of a Greek-style script, similar social practices (a prominent social role for women and the custom of naming children after their mother's maiden name), and common religious ideas and ritual practices (the use of sacred pillars, the worship of a trinity, the predicting of the future by examining the livers of sacrificed animals, and—especially—the Egyptian-style view of an afterlife prepared for with painted tombs).

Another connection linking the Etruscans with the East comes from studies of human blood. In an ethnic group with a long genetic history, the proportion of the four basic blood types remains constant but differs from those of other ethnic groups. Blood studies in modern Tuscany, despite the passage of time and circumstance, reveal that the blood-type constellation of central Italy is markedly different from the blood-type distributions elsewhere in the peninsula. Yet, strikingly, it resembles the blood-type constellation found among the inhabitants of central Turkey today. In addition, the fact that Etruscan civilization appears suddenly in the archaeological soil of Italy suggests transplantation, a theory supported by the fact that the earliest Etruscan settlements lay along the coast, only advancing inland from this beach-head as Etruscan power consolidated.

Another ancient historian, however, Dionysius of Halicarnassus, who lived in the first century B.C., believed that the Etruscans were native to Italy, a theory some modern students of ethnology have taken up. These scholars argue that likenesses between the Etruscans and cultures of the East Mediterranean are due to the fact that these cultures were not taken over by the Indo-Europeans, immigrants who swept down upon the Near and Middle East and Europe in waves soon after 2000 B.C. The Etruscans would thus represent one of a small number of pockets of resistance that maintained their cultural and genetic integrity in various parts of the Mediterranean. Those who argue for this theory also see Etruscan civilization as evolving naturally from earlier Italic cultures.

Of course the Etruscans would be quick to relate their own notion of their origin if they could speak. However, almost no Etruscan literature has come down to us. Unlike Egypt, where a hot, dry climate favors the preservation of scrolls, the climate of northern Italy is too wet and change-able. Thus, if the Etruscans did have a written literature, the scrolls, it would seem, have long since perished.

Etruscan inscriptions themselves are abundant: some ten thousand survive. However, almost all are short. Only about a dozen have more than one line, and almost all are funerary, telling us the name, age, offices, and family connections of the deceased but little else. Only three Etruscan inscriptions contain more than a hundred words, the most curious being the *Zagreb mummy wrapping.* Housed in a museum in Zagreb, Yugoslavia, the Zagreb mummy wrapping is an Etruscan linen scroll that somehow reached Alexandria in ancient times and was used to wrap a Greco-Roman mummy. The scroll consists of a fifteen-hundred-word text and may have been a sacred calendar, although this is in doubt, as we cannot fully decipher it.

Etruscan inscriptions are easy enough to pronounce be-cause the Etruscans used an alphabet based on the Greek, the phonetic values of which are known. However, the lim-ited nature of extant inscriptions makes it difficult to know what most of the words in longer inscriptions mean. We are helped by ancient glossaries from Roman times and by some words the Romans themselves borrowed and bequeathed to us: *histrio* (actor) is the source of *histrionics,* while *antemna* (the yardarm of a ship's mast) lives on in the TV *antenna.* Patient labor by modern scholars using comparative studies has yielded a basic grammar and the probable meaning of about one hundred roots. The consensus of scholars is that Etrus-can is not related to any other known language. If someday we are privileged to find a long bilingual inscription (an Etruscan Rosetta Stone with the same text in Etruscan and a known language such as Latin or Greek), we will have the means to learn much more.

The Etruscans were literate long before the Romans. They were masters of art (sculpture, architecture, and painting), long before the primitive Romans possessed even the rudi-ments of a civilization. Indeed, it was from the Etruscans—masters of central Italy by the sixth century B.C.—that Rome learned lessons that would have a profound effect upon its history. From the Etruscans the Romans learned the meaning of civilization and learned that imperialism could be the way to that better life.

The Etruscan empire was doomed once Rome had learned these lessons. Destruction levels among the ruins of ancient Italic cities confirm what Roman legend relates: the forceful expulsion of the Etruscan overlords. As the Etruscan empire collapsed it was Rome that rose to fill the vacuum of power. Driven from Rome near the end of the sixth century B.C. (the Roman Republic was established in 509 B.C., with the expulsion of the last Etruscan overlord, Tarquin the Proud), the Etruscan league of cities grew progressively weaker in the fifth, fourth, and third centuries in inverse proportion to the growth of Rome's imperialistic success.

The Etruscan response seems to have been one that they were conditioned for by their metaphysical beliefs: a fatalistic acceptance of what the future seemed to hold and what their own sacred scrolls had prophesied—the end of their greatness. Rather than respond aggressively to the Roman challenge, the Etruscans chose ultimately to accept it. Nor were they able to adapt flexibly to the new Roman world. Always rigidly governed by ritual, they cracked rather than bent.

Yet, for the Etruscans it was not merely the real world that had changed, but the world beyond as well. Just as during the heyday of Etruscan power the afterlife had been the bright and glowing reflection of a happy world, so now—as the real world grew darker—the mirrored reflection grew darker too, until it reflected all the brooding anxieties the Etruscans felt. Thus the Etruscans became the prisoners of their own dream, a dream that had become an eternal nightmare.

Artists working in later tombs turned from the bright hues that had been used during Etruria's golden age to cool and somber colors—grays and blues. Haunting images of mazes and monsters appear. Scenes of violence with dripping blood are portrayed—scenes of battle and animal attack (lions against horses or deer) in which the weak and impotent are savagely victimized, a metaphor for the savaging of Etruria by Rome. The repertoire of Greek mythology is called upon for stories of helpless prisoners of war slaughtered and even of brother slaying brother. Vanth, the winged Etruscan goddess of death, and Charu, the hook-nosed, blue-skinned ferryman of the dead, hover nearby as huddled spirits wait. Even the style of interment changed, with the use of sarcophagi for solitary individuals and the use of cinerary urns, both suggesting a weakening in the belief in an enduring afterlife shared lovingly by husband and wife. It is in the eyes of the dead that we can sense the transformation of Etruscan society—a blank, helpless, and sometimes poignant gaze, the death of the Etruscan soul.

The Etruscans, the world's first victims of "future shock," were unable to adapt to a future that hurtled upon them. They left behind neither towering monuments as reminders of the power of their civilization nor even proud inscriptions to recall their national greatness. Conquered and dominated by Rome, their culture was assimilated by their conquerors, as their own unique values shriveled away. Yet their intense love of life, their unwillingness to believe its joys could end, have ensured them the very immortality they sought:

> There is a haunting quality in the Etruscan representations. Those leopards with their long tongues hanging out: those flowing hippocampi; those cringing spotted deer, struck in flank and neck; they get into the imagination, and will not go out. And we see the wavy edge of the sea, the dolphins curving over, the diver going down clean, the little man climbing up the rock after him so eagerly. Then the men with beards who recline on the banqueting beds: how they hold up the mysterious egg! And the women with the conical head-dress, how strangely they lean forward, with caresses we no longer know! The naked slaves joyfully stoop to the wine-jars. Their nakedness is its own clothing, more easy than drapery. The curves of their limbs show pleasure in life, a pleasure that goes deeper still in the limbs of the dancers, in the big, long hands thrown out and dancing to the very ends of the fingers, a

dance that surges from within, like a current in the sea. It is as if the current of some strong different life swept through them, different from our shallow current today: as if they drew their vitality from different depths that we are denied.[25]

10

The Last Moments of Pompeii

The Murmuring Ashes

IT WAS THE VOLCANO that killed her, the volcano she had lived near, too near, until it was too late to run away. Vesuvius killed her, cracked her skull with huge boulders of glowing rock, choked her with subterranean gases until she could breathe no more, until she could only gasp and die, buried in hot ashes twenty-feet deep in that fiery noontime night. Ash wet with rain would harden round her soft body, casting the contours of her breasts before the flesh decayed.

Lush bedrooms lay empty in abandoned villas—the wood of beds turned black with heat, the walls lavished with cracked frescoes of bodies eternally entwined, of passion perpetually consummated. In empty bordellos, graffiti on cubicle walls proclaimed pleasures once known. And everywhere rose the stone phallus, carved on sidewalk and house, symbol of success in a sensual city.

Here they worshiped Venus, the love goddess, and here they died by the thousands on that hot day in August, A.D. 79.

He was seventeen when he saw it happen, saw Pompeii die. His name was Pliny, and he was safe at Misenum, watching from across the shore. In a letter he tells us what he saw:

Wall painting from Pompeii portraying a husband and wife.

The ground was flat, but the wagon they brought us to escape in rocked back and forth despite the stones that blocked the wheels. . . . On the other shore was a black and frightening cloud rent by fiery flashes. . . . Soon the cloud began to descend to earth and cover the sea. . . . Night came upon us, not like a night with clouds or no moon, but like the darkness of a closed room in which every light has been put out. We could hear the wailing of women, the cries of children, the shouts of men: some calling out to their parents, others to their children, still others to their husbands or wives; some in agony over their own fate; others, over the fate of those they loved. Some, frightened to death, begged to die. Many raised their hands to the gods, but more felt there were no gods anywhere. To them it seemed earth's final night. . . . And I, I thought I was going to die with everyone else, and everyone else with me.[26]

Clouds of ash were blown as far as Egypt and Syria. Hushed and shrouded in volcanic dust, Pompeii slept the sleep of ages.

* * * *

The sudden death of a city, the end Pompeii knew, is rare. A lingering death is what most ancient cities knew, dying a little at a time until—impoverished of their original vigor and mature splendor—they turned into ghost towns. History passed them by—as a trade route was abandoned, a river changed its course, a resource failed, or raiders robbed until there was no more.

But history stopped suddenly at Pompeii. Here a city died in the fullness of its vigor, its splendor intact. It is this vitality that sets Pompeii apart from all the other cities archaeologists have unearthed, an insistent vitality that transcends time itself, reminding us that the people of Pompeii were human like ourselves. And how ironic that the very substance that brought Pompeii's life to an end—volcanic ash—should protect the city's soul, permitting it to journey encapsulated through time until it could be reborn.

An entire city survives, a city complete with the common objects of everyday life as it was lived on August 24, A.D. 79. So often archaeologists are only left the arrogant monuments of the mighty—the vaunted halls, triumphal arches, and fortress walls, but here we meet the ordinary people. We see them as though through a series of candid portraits not consciously posed, in photographs snapped two thousand years ago and pressed in an album for us to read—a people "caught in the act of being themselves."

Because of this we can identify with the Pompeiians more than we can with the inhabitants of any single ancient city. Through Pompeii we can understand the Roman past too, on more human terms. We can also come away with something more valuable still, a deeper sense of both the precariousness and the preciousness of our own lives. We may learn to say with the Roman poet Horace: "Carpe diem!" ("Live for today!")

*   *   *   *

Although Pompeii's death was sudden, its rebirth was long and labored. It was rediscovered only in the Italian Renaissance and then only by accident, when Domenico Fontana, an engineer digging a conduit, encountered buildings and street signs naming Pompeii. That was in 1594, after which Fontana's revelations were all but forgotten. Deliberate explorations did not commence until 1758, inspired by discovery of buried antiquities about twelve miles up the coast at the village of Resina, site of ancient Herculaneum. Carried out by order of King Charles III and later by King Ferdinand I of Naples, the explorations at Pompeii were little more than legalized looting intended to satisfy a royal appetite for decorative Classical art on a grand scale.

The science of archaeology—the systematic search for knowledge of the past—was itself still awaiting birth. For archaeologists—the "time diggers"—hunt not gold but the treasures of time itself, the lost but retrievable stories of lives once lived. And these stories can only be read through the careful unearthing and patient reconstruction of every fragmentary page. No chapter can be discarded; no episode torn from its context.

At Pompeii the father of archaeology was Giuseppe Fiorelli. It was Fiorelli who methodically divided the city into excavation zones in the late nineteenth century, required that exacting records of daily progress be kept, and insisted that the whole of Pompeii be treated as a national treasure. His most dramatic innovation involved the scientific "resurrection" of the dead.

As the flesh of the ancient Pompeiians disintegrated, cavities were formed in the ash that surrounded them, cavities that preserved a faithful impression of their bodies. By pouring plaster of paris into these natural molds, Fiorelli created lifelike "statues" of the dead, which revealed not only their anatomy and clothing but even their dying gestures and expressions. Succeeding Fiorelli in excavating Pompeii have been other distinguished archaeologists: Vittorio Spinazzola, Amedeo Maiuri, Pellegrino Claudio Sestieri, and Stefano de Caro.

Excavating Pompeii has not been easy. Pompeii is covered by over twenty feet of pumice and ash, and poisonous volcanic vapors are still trapped in the rooms of Pompeii's hermetically sealed houses, requiring at times that excavators use gas masks. At nearby Herculaneum the problem is compounded by the fact that floods of liquid ash rolled down, creating a sea of volcanic mud forty to sixty feet deep that oozed through and over the city before hardening into concrete. Here "digging" must employ pneumatic drills and water-cooled power saws and proceeds at an excruciatingly slow pace. Moreover, all excavation requires financing, especially difficult in the context of contemporary Italy's precarious economy. Twenty-five percent of Pompeii still lies buried, while at Herculaneum only eight city blocks have been cleared, with eighty percent of the city still underground beneath the modern town that covers it.

Archaeologists must also contend with forces of destruction, both human and nonhuman. In 1943, believing a German panzer division was hiding in the city, the Allies bombed parts of Pompeii. In recent years, with antiquities commanding high prices on the stolen-art market, thieves sawed frescoes off Pompeii's plastered walls, their entry and exit made easier by the fact that this open-air museum lacks a modern security system to guard its perimeter. In November 1980, the earthquakes that ravaged the Naples area caused one hundred cracks, cave-ins, and collapses in Pompeii's ancient structures. And always lurking in the background, that old villain, Vesuvius, not extinct but only dormant, inexorably preparing to erupt again.

Yet on that fateful day in August there was no expectation of disaster. On Vesuvius's gentle and fertile slopes grape clusters ripened in the summer sun. Destructive earthquakes had rumbled in the past, and ominous tremors of late, but for the twenty thousand or more Pompeiians who drank so deeply of life, there was no room for fear.

Seven miles from Vesuvius stretched the city, a neat grid-pattern of shop-lined streets wrapped in a gated wall. Beyond the city lay the glistening sea of Sorrento, Naples, and the isle of Capri.

Pompeii pulsed with industry, the varied aromas of her products filling the air: the odor of urine (used to process felt), the sweetness of shoemakers' leather, the smell of frying olive oil, the pungency of her world-famous fermented fish sauce, and the spiced scent of Campanian wine. Painted wall signs outside the shops proclaimed their wares, while big stepping-stones let pedestrians cross streets to do their shopping clean-footed. Mercury, Roman god of commerce, was worshiped here; "Salve lucrum!" ("God bless profit!") was a Pompeiian prayer.

There were public places for the citizen, such as the Forum and its temples, and places for relaxed pleasure too: at least three public health clubs with swimming pools and steam baths, a music hall, and a theater fitted with jets of perfumed water and a watertight stage for mock sea battles. Twenty thousand could pack into Pompeii's venerable stone amphitheater (oldest in the empire) to watch gladiators fight to the death. There were also fast-food restaurants and taverns that offered pleasures beyond food and drink in rooms upstairs.

Behind the shops that fronted the streets were the two- and three-story private homes of the prosperous merchants. Inside, quiet atriums opened to the sky, and columned interior garden courtyards offered the green tranquillity of nature in the midst of a bustling city. Frescoes framed in rich red decorated the walls and colorful mosaics adorned the floors. High ceilings allowed for coolness in summer. In houses that had few windows, painted landscapes provided imaginary vistas populated with goddesses and heroes from Greco-Roman mythology, some in amorous embraces on bedroom walls. Near one doorway a fierce canine in captioned mosaic warned "Cave canem!" ("Beware the dog!"), while in a dining room a mosaic skeleton with wine pitcher in hand bade banqueters (with unconscious irony) to eat, drink, and be merry before they died.

Through lifelike painted or sculpted portraits, the occupants introduce themselves: the shrewd and perceptive banker, the young lady—stylus touching her lips in meditation, so proud of her literacy—and the young married couple whose large, deep eyes gaze out at us across the centuries. Did they live or die, these ancient Italians? Did they survive or perish in that long terrifying night?

Outside, on the walls of buildings, we can read in Latin the story of their lives. Some messages reveal the practiced hand of the professional sign painter: urging the passerby to vote for a certain political candidate in the upcoming election ("a man of outstanding reputation," or "he'll guard the public purse") or announcing the next gladiatorial games (often sponsored by incumbents). Satirists sometimes countered by appending mock testimonials by drunks, crooks, or the candidate's mistress! One concerned property owner warned: "Sign painter, don't paint anything here. If you put up an election sign, I hope your candidate loses!"

Among the professionally painted signs we also see the scribblings of ordinary people who used the city's walls as bulletin boards. These graffiti (and there are thousands of them) are what reveal the humanity of Pompeii, especially since the most frequent theme is love.

There is bliss: "The only happy man is a man in love"; desire: "I would rather die with you than live as a god without you"; frustration: "What good is it to live with Venus if she is made of marble?"; and resentment: "Lucilla sells her body." Some lovers sent kiss-off messages by wall: "Dear Tertius: You're a slob!" signed, Vergula; or "Alexander, why should *I* care if you don't feel good? I don't care if you drop dead tomorrow!" One philosopher of *amore* wrote, "Lovers are like bees: for them life is honey," only to have a disillusioned reader comment below "If only it were so!"

Among the messages on Pompeii's walls are advertisements by prostitutes. (Appropriate, given that the patron deities of Pompeii were Venus, goddess of love, and Mercury, god of profit.) Among the prostitutes' names we encounter are Fortunata, Successa, Aphrodite, Glycera (Greek for "sweet") and Veneria (derived from "Venus," but here not a medical warning). Panta's name (from Greek for "everything"; hence "You name it!") suggested her erotic versatility.

Prices are given too, although the exact exchange rate we should use to convert prices into dollars is hard to know. The company of the average girl seems to have cost about the price of a modest dinner at a Pompeiian tavern, but some could be had for a lot less, or more. Says one ad outside a hotel: "If you sit down here, read this first: If you're looking for a girl, ask for Attica—four bucks, high-class."

On the walls of the *lupanars (brothels,* from the Latin *lupa,* or *she-wolf)* we even find testimonials from satisfied customers: "Felix did it here twice," and "Placidus got the one he wanted," and at least one not so happy: "Sex is what we came for. The exit is what we want!"

The graphic erotic sculpture of Pompeii, long hidden away in "off limits" rooms of the Naples Museum, and the "how to do it" paintings that decorated the bordello walls prove the carnal dimension of the Italic past. One Pompeiian with apparent knowledge of the Bible summed it up prophetically in a three-word graffito: "Sodom and Gomorrah!"

A Sodom-and-Gomorrah destruction it was, a fiery cataclysm that caught the inhabitants by surprise. The chisel is still in the stone where the sculptor left it; pieces of onyx meant for cameos lie scattered on a jeweler's floor; and the stroke ends where the plasterer ran for his life. Bronze pots and pans are still on the stove; the bones of chicken cacciatore in the casserole; carbonized bread loaves in the baker's oven. Half empty wine cups sit on bar counters, the change still in the till.

From skeletons and plaster manikins of the dead we learn of the victims. Some escaped, only to return to the city to rescue their possessions, and to die. Some embrace one another in the knowledge that death has come; others clutch only material possessions. A beggar lies, the contents of his sack of alms spilled out beside his bony fingers; a skeleton clutches a thousand golden coins that could not buy him life; a mother holds a baby as two older children cling to her dress. Here is a young woman who had lost one shoe in her hurried flight; there is one who stripped off her clothes to run faster—but not fast enough.

Seventeen reside in the Villa of Diomedes: The owner still carries the silver-plated key to his strongbox; his faithful slave still follows behind. Priests lie buried with the sacred treasure they tried to save. A rich merchant embraces the bronze statue he adored.

Some wanted to escape but couldn't even begin. In a prison room near the Forum a skeleton sits with his feet in irons and, in barracks beside the arena, two manacled gladiators who chose the wrong day to rebel. The corpse of a dog is chained to its post; in another house, scattered and gnawed human bones surround a dog that ate its master.

At Pompeii's cemetery a funeral feast was being celebrated inside a tomb. As Vesuvius erupted, a block of stone hurled from the volcano sealed the bronze tomb door, burying the mourners with the dead.

The poignancy of all these lives lost is summed up in a

stanza copied from a wall on the *Via dell'Abbondanza,* the Street of Abundance:

> Nihil durare potest tempore perpetuo
> Cum bene sol nituit redditur Oceano,
> decrescit Phoebe quae modo plena fuit
> sic Venerum feritas saepe fit aura levis.

> All things are transient. The sun after the splendor
> of the day sinks into the ocean, the moon after
> showing us her full light wanes. In the same way
> the anguish of love ends in but a breath of wind.[27]

Soon after this poem was discovered, the plaster beneath it crumbled, and the verses vanished for all time.

Today water gurgles once again from a fountain on the *Via dell'Abbondanza.* Ancient flowers bloom in replanted gardens. Mute voices echo and re-echo their cheers and insults as the wind whispers in the amphitheater. The ashes murmur a timeless song, and for a moment Pompeii is not dead.

11

The Siege of Masada

Defenders of Israel

UP INTO THE DESERT SKY of Judea the smoke climbed from the hot charred timbers of the barricade. Atop the anvil-shaped red rock, poised over a thousand feet above the Dead Sea, all was quiet. Only the steps of the general broke the stillness as he picked his way through the burnt rubble to the interior of the fortress. The Jewish defenders were dead now; the Roman victory, complete.

One hundred years earlier, the rock of Masada (the name literally means *fortress*) had been selected by Herod, King of Judea, as the site for a royal stronghold. Fearing insurrection at home and the foreign ambitions of Cleopatra, he chose Masada because nature had made it virtually impregnable. Set in a wasteland and girded by thirteen-hundred-foot cliffs, Masada could be protected by a small group of defenders against a vastly superior force. On the twenty-acre flat top Herod ordered the construction of a luxurious palace and storehouses to be filled with ample supplies of food and weapons. To provide water in the midst of a desert, Herod ordered the quarrying of huge cisterns high up on the rock. The cisterns, fed by special aqueducts and designed to hold 1.5 million gallons of water, would receive rain from the rare but torrential

Aerial view of Herod's palace atop Masada.

downpours of the desert winter. Despite all these preparations, Herod died in 4 B.C., never having made emergency use of his elaborately contrived bunker.

In the aftermath of civil war that followed Herod's death, a foreign power—the Rome of Augustus Caesar—emerged as the master of Judea. The Roman occupation, however, was met with resistance. In the year 66, during the reign of Nero, this resistance turned to armed rebellion by those who sought freedom from Rome. The war that ensued pitted two chosen peoples against each other: the Jews, who believed their political autonomy was necessary to fulfill their ethical mission in their God-given homeland; and the Romans, who believed it was their divine mission to civilize the nations of the world by organizing them under the rule of Roman law. It was a classic confrontation of East and West, of the militarily irresistible force and the spiritually immovable object. Led by Vespasian and his son Titus commanding the crack Tenth Legion, the Romans moved on the capital city of Jerusalem and besieged it. The temple, used by the freedom fighters as a place of refuge, was captured, ransacked, and burned. It was never to be rebuilt. The western wall of the temple compound, focus for the prayers of later generations of Jews who yearned for the restoration of Zion, still stands in Jerusalem near the mosque that now occupies the temple site. Transported to Rome to be paraded in triumphal procession through the Forum, the looted ceremonial objects can still be seen carved on the ancient marble reliefs of Rome's battered Arch of Titus.

Those Jewish defenders who survived determined never to surrender to Rome and headed south to the fortress-rock of Masada. Early in the war, rebels had surprised a small garrison and seized the fortress, abandoned since Herod's time. It was here that the Zealots decided to make their last stand against the imperialism of Rome.

The Romans meanwhile were otherwise occupied. Nero's death in 68 had left a power vacuum that drew to it a series of coups and countercoups by military commanders hungering to become emperor. The last such commander was none other than Vespasian himself, backed by loyal troops and immensely popular because of his effectiveness in combating the Jewish rebellion. In the year 72, now Emperor Vespasian ordered his governor of Judea, Cornelius Flavius Silva, to march against Masada with the Tenth Legion and terminate Jewish resistance once and for all.

Silva prepared for his siege of the fortress. First he had labor gangs, made up of prisoners of war, build a wall around the base of Masada to ensure that none of the defenders could escape. Next he ordered the construction of a great earthen ramp on the western side of the rock. When the ramp was complete, siege equipment was hauled up into position—catapults for missiles and a huge ninety-foot armor-plated tower containing a massive battering ram to pound down the wall that surrounded the fortress. Finally fire was turned against the defenders, until the wooden shoring used to brace the fortification wall blazed in the night with flames fanned by the desert wind.

What happened next is told to us by a writer named Josephus, a Jew who had first fought in the war against Rome but later changed sides when he sensed the Romans would win. Before the siege of Masada, he had returned with Vespasian to Rome, where he set about writing an account of the war designed to justify his own duplicity by showing the folly of rebellion.

Josephus tells us that the leader of Masada's defenders, Eleazar Ben Yair, urged his followers in words such as these to take their own lives rather than be captured:

> Long ago we decided neither to serve the Romans nor anyone else but God, for He alone is man's true and righteous Lord; and now a time has come that requires we prove our resolve through action. Let us not bring shame on ourselves. In the past we rejected a slavery that would have cost us nothing. Let us not now, in addition to becoming slaves, pay the cruel price we must if we fall alive into Roman hands. . . . Certain is our capture at daybreak, but yet we still have freedom, the freedom to choose a noble death together with our loved ones. This our enemy cannot prevent.[28]

All resolved to do what had to be done. Choking back tears, each man went and slew his own wife and children. Then, after ten men were chosen by lot to be executioners, the rest lay down beside their families and were slaughtered in turn. Finally, Josephus says, the executioners themselves drew lots to determine which one should kill his nine comrades before taking his own life.

When the Romans made their assault the next morning, they were met only by smouldering ruins and silence. Two women, later found hiding with five children in the subterranean aqueducts, told them the story of what had happened.

Though Josephus extols the nobility of the defenders in choosing death, he portrays their choice as the sad consequence of misguided leadership. Thus he has Eleazar regretfully admit in this same speech: "We should have tried to understand God's purpose and realized His once beloved Jewish race had been sentenced by Him to death. . . . This is His vengeance for the many wrongs we were mad enough to inflict on our own people."[29] Thus in a fabricated speech (Josephus was not present at Masada), he has Eleazar acknowledge that rebellion against Rome was wrong.

Indeed Josephus may have even invented the mass suicide. The defenders of Masada may well have fought to the death in defense of principle, but—in a history meant to praise Rome—the conquest of nine hundred and sixty men, women, and children by a ten to fifteen thousand soldier army would hardly have seemed glorious.

What *did* happen on Masada that April day in the year 73? Perhaps we can never know for certain, but because Josephus is our only ancient literary source, it is to the rock of Masada itself that we must turn for more information.

*   *   *   *

Less than twenty years after the founding of the war-torn state of Israel, archaeologists turned for answers to what had been called its "best known unexcavated ancient site." Professor Yigael Yadin of Hebrew University decided to announce the proposed expedition through an advertisement in the London *Observer* in the hope of attracting volunteers to help participate in the dig. The response was overwhelming. Some five thousand people wrote to volunteer their time and labor. The excavation commenced in 1963 and continued for two seasons until April 1965. Hundreds of volunteers came at their own expense from twenty-eight countries and worked under difficult conditions at no pay with only a guarantee of room and board. Digging side by side were chairmen of the board, plumbers, truck drivers, physicians, waiters, lawyers, a shepherdess, a fashion model, and even an elephant trainer!

The expedition encamped in tents not far from where Silva's soldiers had been bivouacked, and they faced many of the same problems the Romans had faced as they had confronted Masada: heat and the logistical problem of providing and maintaining adequate supplies of food and water. Rather than using the dangerous "snake path" on the south face—the only ascent to Masada before its capture—the expedition ascended via the Roman ramp, adding to it stairs built by the Israeli corps of engineers. All in all, ninety-seven percent of the surface of the site was excavated (only the Roman camps and the great cisterns were untouched), and almost two million cubic feet of earth were moved in the course of the excavation.

On the western edge of Masada the excavators uncovered the remains of Herod's thirty-six thousand square-foot palace, the largest building there. They also excavated Herod's Roman-style bathhouse, one of the largest and most ancient of such complexes. It included a dressing room, a cold-water pool, a warm-water pool for bathing, and a hot room, heated by radiant heat through clay wall pipes and a raised floor. Water, splashed on the heated floor, created steam for a steam bath.

At the northern edge of the rock the excavators discovered a three-level luxury "penthouse suite," poised nine hundred feet over the edge of the desert and supported by stone buttresses. Here, on the only portion of Masada blocked from sun and wind, Herod and his guests could enjoy a view of the Dead Sea, the mountains of Moab, the oasis of Ein Gedi, and on a clear day, the city of Jericho. The walls of the penthouse were painted in fresco to create the illusion of rich veined-marble walls.

Herod, a non-Jew, had also built a place of worship atop Masada. During their occupation of the fortress, the Zealots had used the structure as a synagogue, remodeling it by adding two parallel rows of benches for worshipers to sit on. This first-century synagogue, used in the days when the Jerusalem Temple was in ruins, is the oldest known synagogue in the world. Buried in its floor, Yadin's workers discovered portions of two scrolls, one of Ezekiel, the other of Deuteronomy, apparently buried out of piety when they were too worn to be used any longer. Layers of dung found on the synagogue floor suggested it had been used as a stable by the Romans who garrisoned the site after their victory.

The piety of the defenders was also revealed by the discovery of a *mikveh,* or bathhouse for ritual purity, which they had constructed in accordance with Jewish law. Elsewhere on the site, other scroll fragments were found, all requiring delicate handling. The scrolls, made legible through the use of infrared photography, included portions of Genesis, Leviticus, and Psalms. The presence of scrolls used by Jews from nearby Qumran suggested that members of their monastic community had joined the Zealots atop Masada for the final struggle against Rome. The fact that some scrolls had been deliberately destroyed by being torn in many pieces pointed to the spiteful hand of the Roman conquerors.

In sections of the palace and in the space between the casemate wall that surrounded the top of the fortress, the archaeologists found the remains of the cubicles where the defenders had lived: cupboards hollowed out of the wall, simple clay stoves (one with a pot still on it), cooking utensils, measuring cups, a plaited palm-frond basket, a spindle whorl, and clay oil lamps in hollowed-out recesses of walls that still bore smudges from smoke made when the lamps had burned. Portions of wool tunics and bronze belt buckles were also uncovered, as well as signet rings, some of gold.

Ancient beauty aids also were found, used by the women

who occupied Masada: two bronze eye-shadow pencils, a makeup "compact" made of iridescent shell, perfume bottles of clay, a bronze mirror case, and a wooden comb.

In the cubicles and in the storehouses of Herod were found remains of the food the freedom fighters had depended upon, food still preserved because of the heat and dryness of the desert climate: dates and date pits, walnuts, salt, grain, olive pits, and bits of pomegranate. Empty ceramic wine jars were also found inscribed "To King Herod of Judea." Silver and copper coins, of the type made and used during the Jewish rebellion, were also dug up. On them were vine-leaf and wine-chalice designs with Hebrew inscriptions saying "Jerusalem the Holy" and "For the Freedom of Zion."

In the ruins excavators also found hundreds of broken bits of pottery inscribed in Hebrew letters. Among them were eleven potsherds found in a group, written upon in the same hand and bearing the names or nicknames of eleven men, including the name of Eleazar Ben Yair—possibly the very lots Josephus describes as having been used to select the men who would bring death to their fellow defenders.

On the steps leading to a small pool in Herod's penthouse, the excavators came upon a poignant scene: the skeleton of a young woman, sandals at her feet, her brown hair still braided. Near her body was the skeleton of her twenty-year-old husband, clothed in hundreds of silver-plated armor scales. Close to him were the iron heads of the arrows he had once used, one still held to its wooden shaft. With husband and wife was the skeleton of their child.

In a cave near the top of the cliff the bones of twenty-five other individuals were found in disarray, perhaps thrown there by the Romans in the clean-up operation after the fortress's fall. Among the skeletons was that of an old man over seventy years old, and those of fourteen men (estimated between twenty-two and sixty years of age), six young women (between the ages of fifteen and twenty-two), four children (between eight and twelve years old), and the skeletal remains of a human embryo.

These skeletons were given a funeral with full military

honors in 1969. From the evidence that remains, we cannot tell whether these individuals took their own lives or were cut down in a final Roman assault. But either way, there can be no doubt they chose death with honor rather than a life of servitude.

Soon after the completion of the excavations on Masada, the state of Israel issued a commemorative medallion. On one side, framing a depiction of the fortress rock, an inscription in Hebrew and English says, "We shall remain free men." On the back, circled by images of Israel's people, the legend states, "Masada shall not fall again." With equal import new members of Israel's defense forces now take their oath of allegiance atop Masada's heights.

In a scroll found buried beneath the floor of Masada's synagogue are words of the ancient prophet Ezekiel, a prophecy fulfilled by the archaeological resurrection of Masada and by the historic rebirth of Israel:

> And He said unto me: 'Son of man, can these bones live?' And I answered: 'O Lord God, Thou knowest.' Again he said unto me: 'Prophesy upon these bones, and say unto them: O ye dry bones, hear the word of the Lord: Thus saith the Lord God unto these bones: Behold, I will cause breath to enter into you, and ye shall live.'[30]

12

The Dead Sea Scrolls

Scriptures in
the Wilderness

IN 1947, BEFORE archaeologists came to the cave, the Bedouin boy had been there. And before the boy, the stray goat he followed across the cliffs beside the Dead Sea. Higher and higher the two had climbed, until the boy bent down for a stone to drive the goat back. Stretching back his arm, he hurled the stone into the air. Up and up it soared, climbing until its arc crossed the burning path of the sun and the small stone melted in the sun's blinding light.

*   *   *   *

In the year 68, an aged priest had looked up into the same sun scanning the cliff side for his people. As he watched, the white dots that were men shimmered in the desert heat suspended between tan rock and blue sky. Beyond, a haze hung over the salt sea from which no one could drink.

Slowly, ever so slowly, the procession of white-robed Jews ascended the heights of the cliff side, bearing in their arms the linen-wrapped leather scrolls that bore God's word to humankind, the word was the water that could sustain humanity in the driest wilderness.

Cliffs and caves overlooking the Dead Sea at Qumran.

In the second century B.C., the priest's ancestors had been led into the desert by a Teacher of Righteousness. Forsaking Jerusalem where their leader had been persecuted, his followers had come to the shores of the Dead Sea to form a commune of holiness, a remnant of the faithful determined to live in obedience to God's teachings and apart from a world in which evil corrupted good. Here at a place later called Qumran they built their community and spent their days in the purity of scriptural study and prayer, governed by stern discipline and an unbending rule of ethical conduct. Men and women together (some two hundred to four hundred strong), they had come to be saved from evil, but also to wait, to wait for that day when, grown in numbers, the Children of Light would do battle with the Children of Darkness and triumph in the name of the Lord. "Prepare the way of the Lord," the prophet Isaiah had said. "Make straight in the desert a highway for our Lord."[31]

*   *   *   *

Decades passed, but the spiritual army had not grown large enough. And then other Jews decided to act, striking at the Roman oppressors of the first century with guerrilla raids. Eventually the Roman army would lay siege to Jerusalem (and later march on Masada), but so far they had not advanced. Hurriedly, preparations were made to remove the treasures of silver and gold from the temple in Jerusalem and bury them in secret hideaways scattered throughout the land. Because of the piety of the people of Qumran and their isolation, the treasure map, inscribed on copper, was entrusted to them.

Yet even before the Roman army moved against Jerusalem, it moved against Qumran. Now the map itself had to be hidden, as well as the holy scriptures of the community, lest the Romans desecrate and destroy them. With patience, almost six hundred scrolls were carefully wrapped in linen and sealed in pottery jars to be hand-carried to eleven caves high up on the precipitous slopes of the cliffs.

In the year 68 the dreaded Tenth Legion seized and

burned Qumran. By then the men and women of the desert commune may have fled to safety, or may have been killed or taken prisoner. Whatever became of them, they never revealed the places where their holy books were hidden (had the Romans even cared) or the place where they had secreted the map of temple treasure (about which the Romans, had they known, would have cared very much). Even when they garrisoned the site, the Roman soldiers never knew the secrets that were kept in the caves above.

Of the later history of the people of Qumran we know almost nothing with certainty. Some may have died in the defense of nearby Masada, but none ever returned to Qumran. They had been denied a final sanctuary from a violent and avaricious world. For now, the Children of Darkness had won.

*   *   *   *

Arcing out of the blinding orb of the twentieth-century sun, the stone thrown by the Bedouin boy curved slowly downward, dropping and dissolving into the dark mouth of a cave. Then, from the cave opening came a sound, the "ping" of stone striking pottery. His curiosity roused, the boy climbed to the cave, his goat forgotten, and crawled inside.

On the dusty floor stood the ancient jars and their fragile contents just where they had been set some nineteen centuries before. The first of the *Dead Sea Scrolls* had been found.

*   *   *   *

In 1947 political tension was again high in the Holy Land. Trustees over Palestine since the end of World War I, the British were now readying to withdraw and leave it to Arab and Jew to work out their fate. At the very same time, the newly founded United Nations was preparing to vote on whether Palestine should become a Jewish state.

In the midst of this tension, Dr. E. L. Sukenik, professor of archaeology at Hebrew University, received a mysterious call from an Armenian antiquities dealer in Jerusalem. Meeting the dealer at a gateway between the city's military zones, Sukenik was shown a fragment of ancient leather inscribed in Hebrew. Sukenik was told that an Arab antique dealer in Bethlehem had obtained some scrolls from a Bedouin who had found them in a cave by the Dead Sea. Was Sukenik interested in buying them?

On the very day the United Nations prepared for its dramatic vote, Sukenik traveled to Bethlehem to meet with the dealer. In the little shop, the ancient jars that had been found in the cave were shown to Sukenik, and then the scrolls themselves. Later, Sukenik made the following entry in his diary:

> My hands shook as I started to unroll one of them. I read a few sentences. It was written in beautiful Biblical Hebrew. The language was like that of the Psalms, but the text was unknown to me. I looked and looked, and I suddenly had the feeling I was privileged by destiny to gaze upon a Hebrew scroll which had not been read for more than two thousand years.[32]

Sukenik would later purchase the scrolls in behalf of his university shortly before the United Nations decision that led to war between Arabs and Jews.

Only when the Arab-Israeli war of 1948 was over could archaeologists explore the caves of the Dead Sea for more scrolls. Many of the caves had already been ransacked by enterprising Bedouins, but thousands of fragments were still found, and others acquired by purchase. The Bedouins, it seems, had often broken up scrolls that had been found intact in order to multiply their profits by selling the pieces.

The acquisition of the scrolls—however exciting—was the stuff of a palaeographer's nightmare: the crumbling fragments of hundreds of ancient jigsaw puzzles, whose context could only be painstakingly reconstructed on long museum worktables and whose words could often be discerned only with the help of infrared film. What emerged were the parts of the oldest Hebrew Bible we possess, a thousand years closer to biblical days than any other scriptural manuscript previously known.

Although the authenticity of the scrolls was at first challenged by skeptical scholars, the style of script, the shape of the pots, and the carbon-14 testing of the linen wrappings convincingly placed the origin of the scrolls in the first or second century B.C. Until their discovery, the oldest Hebrew Bible had dated back only to the tenth century of the Christian era, antedated only by fourth century Greek or Latin translations.

One of the most curious chapters in the story of the scrolls was written in 1954. In that year, an ad appeared in *The Wall Street Journal* under the heading "Miscellaneous for Sale":

> Biblical Manuscripts dating back to at least 200 B.C. are for sale. This would be an ideal gift to an educational or religious institution by an individual or group. Box F. 206 *The Wall Street Journal.*

Learning of the ad, Professor Sukenik's son, Yigael Yadin—who by chance happened to be in New York on a lecture tour—contacted the advertiser.

As it turned out, the advertiser had been the head of the Syrian monastery of St. Mark in Old Jerusalem. In 1947 he had purchased some scrolls from a Bedouin for about £ 10 each. Unable to find a buyer in his own country, he had traveled to America after the war, tried unsuccessfully for years to find a buyer, and had finally decided to advertise as a last resort. His price: a quarter of a million dollars. Yadin cabled the Israeli government with the proposition. The answer: "Buy."

* * * *

Taken together, the Dead Sea Scrolls now include almost twenty different copies of Deuteronomy and almost as many of Isaiah and the Book of Psalms. Indeed, except for Esther, every book of the Hebrew Bible is in some way represented and in a text and script remarkably similar to the one still used by Jews today.

Discovered also were commentaries on the Bible, prayers of thanksgiving, a Manual of Discipline detailing the people's ascetic way of life, and the War Scrolls, outlining the battle plans for the ultimate spiritual war against the forces of evil. Found also was the temple treasure map, called the Copper Scroll, so badly corroded that it had to be sliced into delicate strips so that it might be laid open. Within, graven in metal, was a list of sixty-four sites where the guardians of the temple had buried sixty-five tons of silver and twenty-six tons of gold! That treasure still remains buried— indeed it may never be found—for the landmarks used as ancient points of reference no longer exist or cannot be identified. Yet, for the men and women of Qumran it would have mattered little, for theirs was a life that put little store in the material things of the world, valuing instead the treasure of God's teachings.

Their pious way of life is borne out by excavations that have been made in the ruins of their settlement. The common rooms where they ate and prayed together and the library where their scribes labored—bent over desks to copy the sacred scriptures—reflect their values. The very desks they used have been found and even the ink pots, dried ink still clinging to them after two thousand years.

Some scholars have seen in the austere life of Qumran parallels to the ways of the Essenes, a monastic Jewish sect referred in ancient histories as having lived by the Dead Sea. A number of scholars have also argued that the Qumran sect influenced the ideas of Jesus, especially his rejection of material possessions and his emphasis upon brotherhood. Edmund Wilson, for example, has declared that "this structure of stone that endures, between the bitter waters and the precipitous cliffs, with its ovens and its inkwells, its mill and its sump, its constellation of sacred fonts and the unadorned graves of the dead, is perhaps, more than Bethlehem or Nazareth, the cradle of Christianity."[33] Yet despite the existence of certain similar beliefs, significant differences also exist, especially in the way in which the people of Qumran defined the spiritual life, not as an active engagement with the world of "publicans and sinners" but rather as a withdrawal from such a world.

How ironic that the first of the Dead Sea Scrolls was found in 1947, shortly before the outbreak of a modern war. How ironic too that the Near East continues to be a region where peace is scarce. Few sanctuaries exist, except among the stars, where one can flee the threat of war; few sanctuaries remain, except within the human heart, where peace can be found.

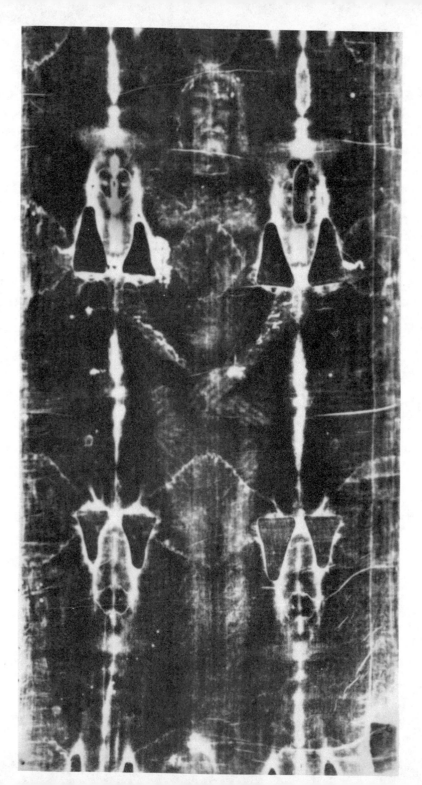

13

The Shroud of Turin

Is This a Photograph of Jesus?

HE HAD STAYED in the church at night long after everyone else had left. Slowly, carefully, he climbed up the scaffold in front of the altar. Atop the platform he leaned over the huge wooden box camera and looked out toward his subject, a sacred cloth suspended in a frame. In the dim light of the cathedral he studied the shadowy, unearthly image of a crucified man, an image imprinted in faint tones on the cloth's surface. It was his church's most sacred relic, and he, Secondo Pia, an amateur photographer, had been chosen to record it on film for the first time. The year was 1898.

Back in his darkroom after midnight, Pia placed the glass negative into the tray of developing fluid. Little by little an image took shape on the plate. Yet when Pia held the plate up to the light he was astounded. Somehow, though this was a negative, it bore the lifelike image of a man with naturalistic highlights and shadows, the very reverse of what a negative should be. Instead, the image looked for all the world like a positive print, with details and features (barely visible on the cloth itself) standing out in bold contrast and relief.

Frontal image of the man of the Shroud as it looks on negative film.

Pia held in his trembling hands what seemed to be an ancient photograph of Jesus.

* * * *

The sacred cloth photographed by Secondo Pia is called the *Holy Shroud of Turin.* Since the sixteenth century it has been kept in Turin, Italy, in the Cathedral of St. John the Baptist. Venerated by many as Christianity's most important relic, it is held by tradition to be the cloth in which the body of Jesus was wrapped when it was taken down from the cross. As Mark tells us (15:46 ff.):

> And when he [Pontius Pilate] learned from the centurion that he [Jesus] was dead, he granted the body to Joseph [of Arimathea], and he [Joseph] bought a linen shroud, and, taking him down, wrapped him in the linen shroud, and laid him in a tomb which had been hewn out of the rock.[34]

The Shroud of Turin is composed of a delicate, hand-woven linen. Its shape is rectangular, about 14'3" long by 3'7" wide. Its color is yellowish, like the color of old ivory. Lengthwise on the cloth can be seen the image of a man's body—actually, a double image: two images, each almost six feet long, joined head to head. One shows the front of a man's body; the other, his back. The double image would have been formed by his back resting on half the cloth, while the cloth's other half was drawn over his head to cover the front of his body. The color of the image can be described as straw yellow or light sepia, not unlike the color of faint scorch marks on an old ironing-board cover.

The earliest historical reference to the Shroud dates to the middle of the fourteenth century. At the time, the Shroud was owned by the Charny family, members of French nobility, and was on display in a church at Lirey, France. Referring to the Shroud as "a certain cloth cunningly painted," a French bishop then declared it a forgery and stated that the artist who had made it had even confessed.

In 1452 ownership of the Shroud passed to the Duke of Savoy, who entrusted it for safekeeping to a church in Chambéry, France. In 1532 a fire broke out in the church. Before the fire could be extinguished, molten silver from the Shroud's casket dropped on the cloth and burned multiple holes through its folded layers. The Shroud still bears watermarks from the fire as well as a series of diamond-shaped patches sewn in by nuns who later worked to repair it. In 1578 the House of Savoy transferred the Shroud to the cathedral in Turin. Upon his death in 1983, former King Umberto II of Italy, a member of the House of Savoy, bequeathed the Shroud to the Catholic Church.

The Shroud of Turin has been exhibited only twice this century: in 1931 (to celebrate the marriage of then Prince Umberto) and in 1978 (the four-hundredth anniversary of the Shroud's arrival in Turin). Rolled in red silk, it now rests in its silver reliquary behind wrought-iron bars under a black marble dome, not to be shown again until perhaps the year 2000, the bimillennial anniversary of Jesus's birth.

Yet, if the Shroud of Turin is the cloth in which the body of the dead Jesus was wrapped, how can one account for the gap in time between the first century, when Jesus was crucified, and the fourteenth, when the Shroud makes its first recorded appearance? If the Shroud cannot be traced back before the Middle Ages, the argument of skeptics is strengthened that the Shroud is a pious forgery like so many other purported "relics" that were called holy and venerated during the Age of Faith.

Compelling circumstantial evidence for the earlier existence of the Shroud has been provided by the twentieth-century French scholar, Paul Vignon. Vignon was struck by the realization that before the sixth century there is no standard artistic conception of Jesus's appearance. In some early Christian portraits, Jesus has short hair; in others, long. Sometimes he is portrayed as bearded; at other times, clean-shaven. The Gospels themselves offer no physical description. Yet in the sixth century a canonical portrait does emerge, one that was consistently followed by later Byzantine and Western European painters. What could account for this single, standardized view of how Jesus looked?

Comparing the face of the man of the Shroud with these later portraits, Vignon discovered that they share over a dozen peculiar and specific features, including a forked beard, locks of hair at the sides of the head, and a curious V-shaped mark or shadow above the bridge of the nose. Vignon theorized that the features of the later portraits derived from the face on the Shroud, that the Shroud had inspired a single canonical view of Jesus's physical appearance. Yet why would such a change have happened in the sixth century?

To be sure, the Shroud of Turin is not mentioned that early by name, but another object is. Called the *Mandylion* (Greek for *cloth* or *veil*), the Mandylion was a cloth that the faithful said bore the imprint of Jesus's face. Tradition said the cloth had been carried from Jerusalem by a disciple of Jesus to the Turkish city of Edessa. Hidden during persecutions, it was secreted in part of the city wall, where it was rediscovered in A.D. 525. Thereafter it became an object of great and mystic veneration and in the year 944 was transferred to the city of Constantinople. After 1204, the year in which Constantinople was sacked by the knights of the Fourth Crusade, all mention of it ceases.

British scholar Ian Wilson has proposed that the Mandylion was actually the Shroud of Turin, folded in such a way that only the facial portion of the image was visible through the opening in its case. The rediscovery of the Mandylion in A.D. 525 and its subsequent veneration would explain why artists, beginning in the sixth century, changed the way they painted the face of Jesus. Because the faces they painted match the face of the Shroud, the Shroud and the Mandylion may have been one and the same.

During the sack of Constantinople, Wilson theorizes, the Mandylion was seized and brought back to Europe by the Knights Templar, who are later described as possessing a mystical image of Jesus's face. One of the Knights Templar was none other than Geoffrey de Charny, a member of the same French family that history records as the first owners of the Shroud.

Thus the Shroud may have journeyed from Israel to Turkey and then to France before its final arrival in Italy. Pollen grains found on the cloth may point to its origin, given that some of them derive from plants that only grow near the Dead Sea.

Yet far more important than the Shroud's journey is the message it bears. What can be seen on the Shroud of Turin? To begin with, one can see the image of a man about 5' 10" in height, whose weight would have been approximately 170 pounds. The details of the body are faintly visible to the eye but become strikingly clear in the high contrast images revealed through black-and-white photography, especially in the series of pictures taken in 1931 by professional photographer Giuseppe Enrie.

Stains of profuse bleeding from the forehead and scalp indicate wounds consistent with the crown of thorns we are told was placed on Jesus's head to mock him as King of the Jews, the pattern of wounds suggesting something shaped like a cap. Welts are visible on the face, reminiscent of the beating Jesus received at the hands of Roman soldiers. Abrasions on the shoulder suggest that a heavy object may have been carried by the man of the Shroud (the cross?). Over 125 lash marks appear up and down the body, front and back. The paired scourge marks match the design of the *flagrum*, the Roman cat-o-nine-tails, fitted with twin thongs ending in metal weights. From the direction and angle of the strokes, we can even deduce that the wielder of the scourge was left-handed. A blood stain on the right side of the victim (with a lighter stain from a postmortem serum flow) recalls how the centurion pierced the side and heart of Jesus with a lance after he had expired.

The wrists and feet of the victim reveal blood flows from puncture wounds like those produced by nails used in crucifixion. The piercing of the wrist as compared with the traditional representation in art of hands pierced reflects the authentic Roman method of crucifixion.

The flesh of the hands is incapable of supporting the weight of a victim's body; instead the Romans drove nails through the wrists whose bones provided the necessary support for the body. The fact that only four fingers of each hand are visible on the Shroud reflects human physiology: injury to the median nerve in the wrist causes the thumb to retract. Furthermore, the direction of blood-flood lines on the arms of the man of the Shroud is consistent with the angle at which the arms would have hung from the cross-beam when the body of the victim slumped from exhaustion. In addition, the stiffness of the buttocks evident on the Shroud's dorsal image demonstrates that the image on the Shroud was produced sometime between one and five hours after death, the period during which *rigor mortis* would have existed.

In summary, the image on the Shroud is anatomically realistic and physiologically authentic. It graphically illustrates the historical realities of Roman crucifixion and the specific sufferings of Jesus enumerated in the Gospels. Yet by what means could this striking image have been produced?

Sophisticated tests of bloodstain marks on the Shroud (light vermilion in color) have now revealed that they are indeed blood, which would have been absorbed into the cloth from the wounds of a victim. If this is indeed the blood of Jesus, it now exists on microscope slides.

But what produced the image of the body itself?

One theory is that the image was made by the absorption into fabric of sweat and unguents, such as olive oil, myrrh, or aloes, used to anoint the body before burial. Close studies of the fibers comprising the body image, however, have revealed no evidence of any substance absorbed by capillary action. Furthermore, bloodstains still in place over various sites of bleeding show that at the time the image was formed the body had not yet been cleansed or anointed.

A second theory proposes that ammonia vapors exuded by the corpse interacted with the fabric and reproduced the image of the body from which they had come. Again, close studies of the fibers have revealed no chemical trace of such vapors. Furthermore, because such vapors would have been diffuse, they could not have produced a body image with sharply defined features. Also, the short period of time within which the image would have had to have been formed—within five hours after death—all but excludes the possibility that sufficiently potent vapors could have been generated by the body.

Could the image then have been man-made? Could it, in short, be a skillful painting?

Intense microscopic studies of the fibers in the Shroud have revealed no trace of any pigment. Paint would have soaked into the threads by capillary action; instead, the fibers are discolored on their uppermost surface only. Analysis has revealed that the discoloration is due to the dehydration of cellulose in the fibers, a type of dehydration characteristic of faint scorching by contact or radiation.

Residual body heat would not have been sufficient in itself to produce such an image. Furthermore, had the image been produced by contact with the body (or with a heated statue, as some have suggested) the three-dimensional molded impression would have produced a distorted image when flattened out, and that is not the case.

Using computer-assisted imaging equipment like that used in the space program to convert digital readouts of light and shadow into contour maps, scientists determined a startling fact: the picture on the Shroud was projected from a three-dimensional source. If we imagine the cloth stretched over the body, we see that the darkest areas of the image are those where the body was closest to the cloth, while the lightest areas are those where the body was farthest away. The closer a given body feature was to the cloth, the more intense an image the body etched upon it. It was the body itself that produced its own image, not through uniform contact but by differential radiation. Using the gradations of light and shadow in black and white photographs of the Shroud, research scientists have been able to reconstruct the contours of the victim's face and physique.

Computer analysis also revealed that the image on the Shroud is totally nondirectional; that is, it was not produced by the movement of a brush or other device. Instead, the image on the Shroud resembles, upon close inspection, a dot matrix. Apparent gradations in density do not result from some fibers being darker than others but rather from a higher concentration of darkened fibers in a particular area.

Two unnaturally raised areas on the eyes attracted particular attention when three-dimensional models of the face were studied. Some theorized that the raised areas represented coins placed over the eyes of the deceased to keep his lids closed. A comparison of these areas with the coins of Pontius Pilate revealed that they were consistent with the coins' size and shape. A computer-enhanced three-dimensional enlargement of these areas, under the direction of Father Francis Filas of Chicago's Loyola University, produced a startling revelation: the outlines of the very symbols used on the ancient coins (a staff and a shock of wheat) and the letters U CAI at one coin's edge, letters from the actual ancient inscription, TIBERIOU CAISARIS, named the emperor, Tiberius Caesar, who ruled the Roman world in the days of Jesus.

With all this evidence, it is difficult to conceive how the image of the Shroud could have been made by an artist. If the image on the Shroud was man-made, the artist would have had to possess an understanding of human anatomy and physiology. He would have had to know the Roman method of crucifixion and had access to Roman coins dating to the days of Pontius Pilate. He would have had to produce an image that duplicates a photographic negative, an image of a man that would only become fully visible and natural with the aid of photography. He would have had to include details visible only through the use of three-dimensional computer-imaging devices. And he would have had to possess the technical means to produce such an image by radiation scorching.

On the grounds of physiological and historical knowledge alone, the picture could not have been produced in the Middle Ages. A comparison with the depiction of the crucifixion by medieval painters demonstrates how the image on the Shroud surpasses their work in realism.

If the image was made by an artist, the artist would have lived in the first or second century of the Roman period, a time when portraiture was realistic (witness the mummy portraits of the Egypt's Fayum district and the paintings of Pompeii), and when an accurate knowledge of crucifixion practices would have still existed. (Crucifixion, practiced tens of thousands of times by the Romans against political rebels, was not stopped until the fourth century.)

But such a Roman date still does not explain how such an artist would have produced the image or why it would have been produced in a manner that would not allow its appreciation until the development of photography.

To explain what radiant source of energy burned the image of the man of the Shroud into the cloth, some have proposed the process of resurrection itself, an event in which flesh would be transformed into spiritual energy. If this is so, the image on the cloth would constitute a photograph of Jesus taken at the moment of resurrection.

In recent times the Shroud has been subjected to a variety of sophisticated laboratory tests, "some of the most exhaustive research ever conducted on any relic, object of art, or archaeological artifact."[35] Though a 1988 carbon-14 test of a fabric sample dated it to between 1260 and 1390 A.D., the procedures used for the test have been criticized on scientific grounds. Nor would any date in itself, medieval or otherwise, explain how the mysterious image on the cloth was produced. The one certainty is that "as more questions are answered, more arise."[36]

Ironically, the Shroud seems to become more inscrutable as time passes. Recent researchers have marveled at how faint the image seems (it virtually disappears to the eye at closer than three feet and farther than six), and how its color seems paler than one would conclude from earlier descriptions. Could it be that the image on the Shroud is fading away? Is it possible that when the cloth is unfolded in the year 2000 the image may well be altogether gone? How ironic that as science draws closer, the image on the Shroud withdraws.

Perhaps someday science will be able to explain the Shroud in a way that precludes the concept of a miracle. Until such a day, the most moving commentary will remain that of French writer Paul Claudel: "Something so frightening yet so beautiful lies in it that a man can only escape it by worship."[37]

14

Early Christianity in Rome

Echoes from the Catacombs

HIS NAME was Dalmatius. He was not yet seven years old. Yet he had learned the Greek alphabet, and, although he had no teacher (his parents were too poor to afford one), he had taught himself to write Latin too. He was wise beyond his years, filled with a promise that brightened his father's life. Then in three days he was dead, and darkness fell over his father's life. They buried the boy outside Rome eighteen centuries ago.

*   *   *   *

Ancient Roman law forbade burials within the city limits. And so it was that the Romans for centuries had buried their dead at the city's outskirts. Along stone-paved highways like the Appian Way that radiated from the empire's capital, tombs were erected to honor families of distinction. The weary traveler, pausing on his journey, would keep their memory alive by contemplating the sculpted portraits affixed to their sepulchers, reciting the litany of their names.

The long-persecuted Christians also had buried their dead along these roads. The soft subsurface rock, known as tufa,

Staircase leading down to the catacombs of St. Callixtus, Rome.

was easy to quarry and allowed the excavation of underground burial sites. Here, large-scale inexpensive burials could take place for those of modest means, the underground location protecting their graves from desecration. The use of such communal cemeteries also allowed the dead to be buried as a group so that they might together find eternal peace and await resurrection.

These cemeteries came to be called *catacombs,* though the origin of the word is obscure. It seems to be Greek, the language of the eastern Roman Empire and the Gospels. The word may have meant "down by the tombs" (because of the nearness of the catacombs to pagan sepulchers) or "the hollows" (in reference to the low-lying land that formed the site of the oldest and best known of the Christian cemeteries, the catacomb of St. Callixtus).

No one today knows how many catacombs exist in Rome (many surely still lie buried), but almost fifty have been identified. It has been estimated that these contain perhaps a hundred miles of underground passageways and nearly a million graves.

Steps lead down to narrow corridors twenty to twenty-five feet below ground. Along the walls of these corridors are six-foot-long niches called *loculi,* carved out of the bedrock to hold the bodies of the dead. To make maximum use of this wall space the burial berths were tiered—two-, four-, or even twelve-high. Each opening was bricked and plastered after burial; a tablet was then added, bearing the name and age of the deceased. In special cases an arched vault might be added. Some families preferred to be buried in a family crypt, or *cubiculum,* a large chamber with the bodies of family members set in walls or flooring.

Channels called light-wells were sometimes dug to the surface to allow daylight to penetrate the otherwise dark passageways and chambers. As the need for additional space grew, lower galleries were added, connected to the upper passageways but sunk as much as sixty to seventy-five feet below ground level.

In the subterranean darkness the colors of paint illuminate

the lives once lived by the early Christians. The paintings, done on the plastered surfaces of the cubicles and on ceilings and walls, are the oldest Christian paintings we possess. Although they are not impressive as fine art—those who painted them were often humble artisans—they are extraordinary as testaments to the faith of the early Christians, "a faith," as E. R. Goodenough has said, "much simpler and more direct than the faith of the involved theologies of the time."[38] Another commentator has fittingly described them as "a pictorial translation of prayer."[39]

Like the catacombs themselves, the paintings begin in the second century A.D. They employ many potent symbols of early Christianity: the dove, symbolizing God's protection; the anchor, symbolizing the security that comes from faith; the superimposed Greek letters *chi* and *rho*, the first two letters of Christ's name in Greek; and the fish, the spelling of which in Greek contains the first letters of the words for "Jesus Christ, son of God, Savior." The most frequent image is that of Jesus as the Good Shepherd, holding on his shoulders a lamb. The faithful are symbolized as worshipers with hands upraised in prayer.

Stories are also found in the paintings of the catacombs. Strikingly, there are far more subjects that derive from the Old Testament than the New, perhaps because of early Christianity's closeness to Judaism. Many pictures portray the theme of deliverance, of urgent import in an age of persecution. Noah waits prayerfully in the ark; the Israelites cross the Red Sea; Daniel stands in the lion's den, and Shadrach, Meshach, and Abednego in the fiery furnace—scenes of torture the likes of which Christian martyrs had known at the hands of their pagan persecutors. The story of Jonah reminded the faithful that God's power could reach westward across the Mediterranean and that those who turned to Him would be shown mercy.

In addition, the catacomb paintings provide us with the earliest surviving depiction of the Virgin Mary and the infant Jesus. Jesus himself is also portrayed, usually as a young man, clean-shaven and dressed in Roman garb. Scenes of

Jesus's life, however, only rarely appear in the catacombs before the time of the third century. The Sermon on the Mount is depicted only once. Far more frequent are scenes of Jesus working miracles, especially the raising of Lazarus from the dead, an episode that would have inspired the early Christians with hope for their own future resurrection. Baptism and communion meals are also frequent subjects, with bread and fish rather than bread and wine being used to celebrate the Eucharist. It is striking that the crucifixion does not appear as a theme in Christian art until the fifth century, when it is used for the first time on a sarcophagus.

The paintings of the catacombs also reveal the rootedness of many of the early Christians in the pagan culture of Rome. In some of the paintings we can recognize figures from Greco-Roman mythology: the lovers, Eros and Psyche, and Helios, the god of the sun, riding in his heavenly chariot. Even the Good Shepherd recalls Classical images of the hero, Orpheus, and the Greek god, Hermes.

From the inscriptions that accompany the paintings and from pictorial clues we can also learn about the occupations of many of those who were buried in the catacombs. Along with the bishops of the early Church are also a vegetable seller, a barrel maker, a wagon driver, a hauler of grain, a baker, an ivory merchant, a perfume seller, a soldier, a chariot racer, and even a gladiator—a demonstration of the broad spectrum of people whose lives the Christian faith moved and who often died as martyrs to that faith.

Side by side with the inscriptions and paintings are graffiti, left by pilgrims for whom in later centuries the catacombs became a shrine. When in the fourth century the Roman emperor Constantine stopped the persecution of Christianity, turning to it instead to provide spiritual renewal for Rome, churches were built and churchyard burial introduced. Gradually the catacombs fell out of use. In the midst of barbarian raids and the disorder of the Dark Ages, many bodies were reburied in churchyards and relics taken to Rome for safekeeping. By the tenth century the catacombs lay unused, their entrances overgrown and forgotten.

It was not until the days of the Italian Renaissance that the catacombs were rediscovered, chiefly through the efforts of a young Maltese named Antonio Bosio, who by following pilgrims' guidebooks single-handedly identified the sites of thirty catacombs, earning for himself the name "the Columbus of the Catacombs." In the nineteenth century, the age of scientific archaeology's birth, the catacombs were carefully explored and examined by Giovanni Battista de Rossi.

Among the catacombs Bosio had found was a Jewish one. By the early twentieth century, six more had been discovered. Only two have survived deliberate destruction, and only one of these is still accessible. In the Jewish catacombs Hebrew inscriptions are rare. Except for the frequent use of *Shalom* (the Hebrew word for "peace"), inscriptions are almost always in Greek, the common language of the East. As was true of the Christian catacombs, pagan symbols are also evident here (sea horses, dolphins, cornucopias), but it is the symbols of the Jewish faith that abound: the *menorah* and the *shofar* (the candelabrum and ram's horn), the ark of the covenant with the scrolls of the Torah, and the festive palm branch and citron. Inscriptions give the names and occupations of the dead as well as the special offices they held in their synagogue. In some cubicles skulls, bones, bits of linen shrouds, and objects of gilded glass remain. On the walls of the cubicles the stains of myrrh and aloes, once used to anoint the dead, can still be seen.

In some Christian catacombs objects were placed in the mortar when the niche was covered over: a coin, an oil lamp, a small doll, a child's toy. In the now-empty space of a small niche a young boy's body once lay. Here a father's tears were shed so many centuries ago as he left his hope behind in the darkness. The inscription recalling that time remains:

> To Dalmatius, my son, my dearest,
> so gifted, so wise,
> boy whom an unlucky father could only cherish
> for less than full seven years,
> who could write in Greek,
> who picked up Latin by himself

> who in the space of three days
> was snatched from our lives.[40]

The poignant letters can still be traced with our fingers as Dalmatius's father once traced them, there in the darkness, so many centuries ago.

15

Portraits from Roman Egypt

The Faces of Fayum

THEY CALLED HIM Artemidorus. The name was Greek and Greek was his mother tongue, but all the same, Egypt was his home. Of course, even Egypt was no longer the Egypt it once had been, since Assyrians and Persians, Macedonians and Romans had come to rule the land. And yet, Artemidorus knew in his heart that Egypt *would* always remain Egypt: the Nile and desert would never change their face no matter how many conquerors came. In the end the old would prevail, nature over civilization, the millennia absorbing the moment into themselves until it was no more. If one pondered it, Artemidorus sometimes thought, the world could seem a very confusing place, but his philosophy gave him peace.

Centuries before, another Greek had come to the land—Herodotus, traveler, maker of history, teller of tales. He had looked and questioned, amazed by the Egypt he saw, intrigued by its contradictions. But Herodotus was only a tourist, if a curious one at that. Egypt was a nice place to visit, but Artemidorus had to *live* there. For him there was far too much sand (it seemed to be everywhere) and a sun that always seemed too hot.

But it wasn't a bad country for all that. He lived in Arsinoë, known to some as Crocodilopolis, home of the sacred

Portrait of Artemidorus, from his mummy case.

crocodile and capital of a district called the Fayum. The soil was fertile and water plentiful. Many veterans had come here to live after serving in the armies of Ptolemy or Caesar, and much land had been reclaimed just for them. Busy merchants were here too and bustling bureaucrats.

One hundred fifty miles to the north lay Alexandria, a great and vital city, with a rich cultural life. Even though its famous library had been damaged by fire, its great lighthouse, the Pharos, seventh wonder of the world, still shone as a beacon to Europe. Here lived revered scholars and poets. Here was the tomb of Alexander the Great, founder of the city that bore his name, and the grand palace where, two centuries ago, Julius Caesar and Cleopatra had met.

The second century A.D., Artemidorus's time, was an era when Roman civilization was most blessed in arts and learning, material comforts and liberty. All the styles eventually came to Alexandria from Rome: the latest fashions in clothes, the latest coiffures, the latest manners. It took time, but they came, for if Rome was emperor of the world, surely Alexandria, seat of the wealthiest of Rome's provinces, was the queen of the Mediterranean.

Like so many of his upper-class friends, Artemidorus was having his portrait painted for display in his home. On a thin wooden panel, about 13 by 15 inches, the artist had first applied a coating of plaster and then sketched in his subject's face. Next would come the colors drawn from mineral pigments: black from lamp soot, yellow from ocher or orpiment (a compound of arsenic), blue and green from malachite and azurite, and red from ocher or lead, all blended into molten wax. Artemidorus was fascinated by the use of the wax and how the painter worked his heated colors until he could apply them with spatula and brush to the surface of the wooden panel. The hues seemed so lustrous and deep.

Artemidorus knew that after his death the painting would be taken down from the wall and placed over the face of his mummified body. He had lived in Egypt so long now that he had come to accept many traditions that at first had seemed strange. He could anticipate the day when his body would be embalmed in accordance with ancient custom and swathed in bandages to be placed in a case decorated with the gods of the afterlife. Framed in gold leaf, a golden wreath across his head, he would look out—shoulders turned three-quarters, head just a bit less, just as the painter had posed him—his dark brown eyes gazing at those who might later look at his face and wonder who this man had been.

Why should a Greek not choose this way? Did not the Egyptians say man could find eternal life and happiness after death, something the dankness of his own Greek Hades had never offered? And could one not see in the gods of Egypt and Greece likenesses and common truths?

Through his portrait he would always appear in the prime of life, always youthful, the flame of his soul never wavering and always burning bright. A Greek inscription would someday be added in final tribute by the family he loved: "Artemidore Eupsychi," "Artemidorus, Farewell."

*   *   *   *

Light shone once again on Artemidorus's face in the nine-teenth century, for it was then that his tomb was discovered. In a brick-lined family crypt buried beneath the sands for seventeen centuries, his mummy case was found. Beside it was the body of another Artemidorus (his father, perhaps, or son) and the body of a woman named Thermoutharin (his mother, perhaps, or sister, or wife). Today the portrait of Artemidorus, along with his mummified body, rests in London's British Museum.

His portrait is one of almost six hundred such paintings done in the encaustic (hot wax) technique used in Roman Egypt. Dating to between the first and fourth centuries A.D., they are collectively known as *Fayum* portraits from the modern name of the region in Egypt where the vast majority have been found. The largest caches were uncovered in 1887 by Viennese antiquarian and art dealer Theodor Graf and in 1888 and 1911 by archaeologist Sir Flinders Petrie, chiefly from the cemeteries of such Hellenistic enclaves as Arsinoë and Philadelphia, the latter named for one of Egypt's benevolent Ptolemaic rulers, Ptolemy II Philadelphos.

The portraits reflect what must have been a very popular art form in the days of the Roman Empire. Similar portraits, painted in fresco on the walls of private homes, survive in Pompeii or Herculaneum, but the bulk of such pictures has perished for want of the right environment to preserve it.

The faces of Fayum seem to us astonishingly real. This is attributable to the enduring richness of the colors and the facility of the artist in creating the illusion of three-dimensionality through skillful shading and highlighting. But such realism is also due to the very thrust of Hellenistic and Roman art, which, at its best, sought to communicate the full humanity and distinct individuality of its subjects. Occasionally we know from inscriptions the names of those portrayed and, sometimes, even their occupations. Thus we can number Demetris, Demos, and Hermione the Schoolteacher among our friends.

Today they live in museums around the world: in Cambridge and Carlsberg, in Brussels and Brooklyn, in Edinburgh and Detroit. Perhaps no better group of immigrants could have been selected for such transplantation: Levantine citizens of the world, they understood what it meant to make a new home. Today, even as we stand before them, their dark eyes contemplate us in turn, bidding us to remember they are not dusty exhibits in a museum of things, but real people from a world that once was.

*   *   *   *

The everyday lives of the people of ancient Fayum are revealed through the miracle of papyrus. Since their occupation of Egypt, the Greek and Roman residents had used native papyrus as their regular writing material. Beginning in the late eighteenth-century, European antiquarians acquired fragments of such manuscripts, though we are told precious quantities were lost, set afire by Egyptian peasants who liked "the aromatic smell they gave forth in burning."[41] Following a major find at Arsinoë and later discoveries made by Petrie at nearby Hawara, a British expedition was financed specifically to search for such papyri. The leaders of the expedition, B. P. Grenfell and A. S. Hunt, were to work as a team for years in the Fayum and farther south at Oxyrhynchus.

The papyri they found came from a variety of sources: the ruins of houses, the rubbish heaps of offices, and the garbage dumps of towns. Grenfell and Hunt also discovered papyri in unexpected places. Papier-mâché mummy masks and breast covers from the Greco-Roman period were found to consist of layers of discarded but legible papyri, often belonging to the same batch of ancient correspondence. Examining the interior of mummified crocodiles, they even found intact papyrus scrolls, inserted by the priests into the empty crocodile bodies to help them keep their shape.

Among the materials discovered were very early copies of the Gospels and a moving collection of sayings attributed to Jesus. Classical writings were found as well, including pages from Homer and lost poems of Sappho.

In the baskets full of fragments Grenfell and Hunt were to accumulate, other seemingly more trivial documents were gathered, but collectively they recount the rhythms of everyday existence in Greco-Roman Egypt. Such papyri testify to the lives of ordinary people, lives that are unrecorded in the larger monuments of the past.

There are marriage contracts and decrees of divorce, census records and wills, tax receipts and bills of sale. There are invitations to birthday parties, weddings, and dinners ("Come at nine!"). There are letters too.

A husband, working in Alexandria, writes home to his worried wife, pregnant with their second child and close to delivery. A man tries to hire three castanet dancers (Isadora and her friends) for a party at his home. A penitent son appeals to his mother for one more loan. A soldier newly stationed in Italy reassures his family in Egypt that all is well. Orders are given to roll out the red carpet for a visiting VIP from Rome. And reimbursement from a landlord is requested for costs attendant upon the hiring of a professional mouse catcher.

These pieces of papyrus give us a new perspective too, for they teach us how uncertain a thing life was to the people of the past. Though *we* know from our history books how the world would turn out, *they* did not. And though we measure out the cloth of history in the yardage of kings and conquests, the fabric of their lives was woven of a finer thread.

We see this in a fragment found at Oxyrhynchus, dating to A.D. 300. The fragment is a partial list of queries once put to an Egyptian oracle. In its inventory of personal questions we hear the anxious voices of long ago:

"Shall I stay where I am going?"

"Am I to be sold as a slave?"

"Will I be reconciled with my child?"

"Shall I get the money?"

"Will I be able to do what I intend?"

"Am I to become a senator?"

"Will I go broke?"

"Am I to be divorced from my wife?"

"Have I been poisoned?"

"Will I get what I want?"

Sleep well, children of Fayum. No longer need you worry over the answers the oracle would give. Sleep well in the peace that only death can bring.

16

The Story of Roman Britain

At Rome's Frontier

FOR SIXPENCE CHARON will row you across the Almond. And they come—Sunday lovers, babies, and clerks—waiting on salt-sprayed wooden steps in the sun. The north shore of Cramond teems now: three-year-olds feel the cool mud of rolling banks ooze through their toes; a thick-legged woman, one child under each arm, balances on boulders, making for the sea; and upriver, green-sheltered from the plash of rapids, a swan, drifting in a slow spin, plucks fleas from its down.

The fort is in the churchyard—or what remains of the fort. Now brick and gravel, left by the diggers, mark where foundations of storehouse, workshop, and barracks once stood. Here on the Scottish coast in A.D. 142, beyond the great wall Hadrian had stretched across Britain, a fort was built to guard a vital line of supplies. To the north lay the threat of barbarian invasion; to the south, the continuity of Roman peace. Here at Cramond, a few miles west of Edinburgh, the fort was to stand, to be evacuated and then destroyed by the enemy, to be rebuilt and garrisoned into the fourth century, and then, in a slowly Christianizing world, to become the site of a church whose descendant now abides on ground where once a Roman commander sat and made his plans.

Five miles away, the bronze and silver coins, rubbed

Portrait of the Roman emperor Hadrian discovered in the Thames.

smooth with use but still showing the cool faces of passionate emperor and empress, lie in the glass case of an Edinburgh museum. Fragments of red-glazed pottery used by officers (on one a lion bites the leg of a stag) survive, and stone vessels once filled to make soldiers' meals. A Cupid in clay, a broken brooch, and the upturned face of a dice cube tell of life in the fort and in the small village that grew up beside it, a life now lost but once, like our own, lived out in the present.

In an age that Edward Gibbon called the one "during which the condition of the human race was most happy and prosperous,"[42] life at Cramond could be simple, stern, and short. The feel of coarse bread, the smell of latrines, a watch in the cold, damp night: these were the cement of hours for men sometimes a thousand miles or more from home. And if a sentry had memories, they were not of mighty Caesar or the grandeur of Rome—rather perhaps of warming Italian wine, a bed less hard, the face of that girl in Londinium.

* * * *

Before the Romans, there *was* no London. The first Roman general to cross the English Channel was Julius Caesar. Fearing that British tribesmen might ally with their Celtic brethren in Gaul, Caesar made two forays onto English soil, in 55 B.C. and again—with a more massive show of force—the following year. The Romans were not to return for almost a century, but when they came next they came to conquer. In the reign of the emperor Claudius, made famous by Suetonius and Robert Graves, the Roman eagle finally spread its wings over England.

The conquest was not without resistance. At an earthwork fortress called Maiden Castle, two miles southwest of Dorchester, the Roman army attacked a rebellious tribe. From the archaeological remains we can reconstruct the scene:

The Roman infantry, covered by a barrage of iron-shod ballista-arrows, fought their way up to the eastern gate. Some huts had been built here outside the actual gateway;

the Romans set them on fire and, masked by the smoke, stormed the gates, burst into the town and started a massacre of the inhabitants. Then they dismantled the gates, tore down the palisades and withdrew to their camp leaving the survivors to bury under cover of night the bodies of those that had fallen; nineteen centuries later the excavators were to find those graves, hastily dug in the hot ashes of the huts outside the ruined gateways.[43]

In this earliest of English war cemeteries, the skeletons themselves tell their story. A woman, killed by three blows to the head, lies with her arms bent behind her body as though they had been bound at the time of her death. Two men lie buried together. The skull of one is pierced by a square-headed projectile, probably a bolt from a Roman catapult. Between the vertebrae of the other an iron arrowhead is jammed, having entered the chest below the heart. A sword cut to the head, still marked in the skull, finished him off.

About the time Maiden Castle was stormed, Roman engineers had already selected the site for a bridge across the lower River Thames. The commercial settlement that grew up at that crossing, Londinium, soon became the center for Roman trade and administration, and eventually grew to be the largest and richest of settlements in Roman Britain.

The mud of the Thames bears evidence of London's rise. The very timbers have been found that once formed a wooden foundation-pier for the Roman bridge. Today's London Bridge is located close by the ancient site. Old London Bridge, built in 1831, now curiously crosses a portion of Lake Havasu, Arizona, having been purchased and transported in 1968 by American industrialist and developer Robert P. McCulloch for a little less than ten million dollars.

Near the site of ancient Roman wharves in London, archaeologists came upon the wooden hull of a Roman freighter. In the socket of its mast was a Roman coin put there for good luck by the captain. Fittingly, the coin shows the goddess of good luck, Fortuna, holding the rudder of success.

The protective mud of the river has also offered up a

bronze helmet with conical "horns" once worn by a British tribesman and a gilded bronze shield inlaid with red glass. Rediscovered where it had been hurled with anti-Roman fury is a second-century portrait-head of the wall-building emperor Hadrian, ripped from the bronze torso to which it had once been attached.

London itself presents particular problems to the archaeologist. As a city that has had a continuous existence for almost two thousand years, London hides its past beneath its streets. Could today's London be peeled away (a most unlikely event), we would see the remains of Elizabethan, medieval, and Roman London layered beneath.

Ironically, it is the future that discloses the past: when foundations are dug for new buildings, older strata are revealed. This is especially true in the case of high-rise structures with deep foundations and multiple basements. Even wanton destruction can reveal the past: the World War II bombing of London produced deep craters that reached into ancient depths.

Today we know the location of the Roman governor's house and the site of the city's forum. In the basements of some of London's modern shops and office buildings, carefully preserved Roman foundations and mosaic floors can be visited by special appointment.

Perhaps the most remarkable construction-site find was a temple dedicated to the god Mithras. A Persian god who offered worshipers eternal life, Mithras was one of the most popular gods of the ancient world, especially with soldiers of the Roman army. In the ruins of the temple were found a sculpted head of Mithras, an ornate silver jar and strainer, and a magnificent marble portrait of the bearded Greco-Egyptian god Serapis. These objects had been buried for safekeeping by fearful priests after their temple had been attacked, possibly by rival Christians.

Other artifacts from Roman days have been found beneath London's streets: leather shoes (including hobnailed boots and multistrap sandals); a curious leather bikini bottom; hairpins and tweezers; a lady's comb carved with her name (Modestina); an inkwell; wooden writing tablets (once coated with wax) and styli (to scratch on the message); coins by the hundreds; tradesmen's tools; and an officer's sword and metal sheath, the latter embossed with a picture of the Roman she-wolf nursing Romulus and Remus. In the ruins of a Roman bath, a pavement was found still imprinted with the footprints of a child who had walked across the cement before it had dried.

Standing on a street corner in London today, we can shut our eyes for a moment to imagine what a street scene in Roman times would have been like:

> Farm-carts, troops of soldiers, mounted messengers would pass and re-pass. Smoke would be rising from the furnaces of public baths; there would be the hum of life; carts and chariots rattling along the streets, the distant shouts of stevedores and sailors unloading ships at the wharves, the ring of smiths' anvils; and the staccato yelp of saws from the artisans' quarter. . . . The picture fades; and there is the tight huddle of banks and commercial offices, the new glass and concrete skyscraper blocks, and the red buses crawling past St. Paul's.[44]

For relaxation the wealthy of Roman Britain could resort to Bath, one hundred miles west of London. The Romans, who had always reveled in the sensual stimulation and social interaction of communal baths, were delighted by the discovery of naturally heated mineral springs at this Celtic village, the only source of such waters in all Britain. Soon the village was transformed by Roman engineers and architects into a luxurious spa generating five hundred thousand gallons of water a day, warmed by nature to a temperature of 120 degrees. The rectangular Great Bath measured 40 by 80 feet and, when excavated in the nineteenth century, was still covered with its original waterproofing—sheets of British lead weighing forty pounds each. Jutting out at one end of the pool was a large stone from which the bathers dived, its surface worn hollow by centuries of divers' feet.

To the north of London and Bath were the legionary forts

that served as the bases of Roman power, and the settlements that grew up around them, settlements whose names —like Chester and Colchester—echo the word *castrum*, the Latin name for "fort." The well-to-do might live in villas, like one at Fishbourne, furnished with elaborate gardens and mosaics, and use exquisite silver plate, like the treasure turned up at Mildenhall by a farmer's plough during World War II. Buried in the fourth century to protect it from Saxon raiders, the silver service included an eighteen-pound silver dish measuring almost two feet in diameter and decorated with a scene celebrating the triumph of Bacchus, god of wine.

For entertainment some towns offered Roman-style drama performed in theaters, such as the impressive one that survives at St. Alban's (ancient Verulamium), twenty miles north of London. When such drama went out of style in the late fourth century, the outdoor theater unceremoniously became the town dump. A clay roof-tile from St. Alban's still preserves a bit of real-life drama. While the clay was laid out to dry, a dog decided to walk across it. Seeing what was about to happen, the tilemaker shouted and, in desperation, threw a stone in the dog's direction. The baked tile still bears the imprint of the dog's paws and the hole made in the clay by the errant stone.

Far to the north, linked by a network of Roman roads to supply depots and garrisons, stands Hadrian's Wall. Planned by the emperor himself during his visit to Britain in A.D. 122, the wall was designed to protect Romanized Britain from barbarian invasion. (The barbarians, in this case, were the intractable Scots!)

More than a wall, Hadrian's Wall was an elaborate system of defense. Running east and west for seventy-two miles from the Tyne to the Solway Firth, Hadrian's Wall incorporated sixteen full-sized forts (one about every five miles), smaller forts called mile castles at mile intervals, and lookout turrets every half-mile. The wall was fronted by a high mound and a deep V-shaped ditch designed to blunt a charge by the enemy and make attackers easy targets for archers stationed on the wall's heights. Pairs of sally ports, located at strategic intervals, permitted Roman soldiers to exit on the north side and form pincer movements, driving the enemy into the wall itself where death waited.

In the east, the wall was built fifteen feet high; in the west, where rugged natural terrain itself made attack difficult, a height of only twelve feet was required. When the wall was first constructed, Hadrian ordered that its sections be built by the very men who would be stationed to defend them. Knowing their own lives would depend on their skillfulness, the legionnaires built well (an intriguingly effective method of quality control). With good reason, long sections of the wall still traverse the English landscape.

Twenty years later, in A.D. 142, a territorially more ambitious wall was built to the north in Scotland, the so-called Antonine Wall, traces of which can still be seen near Edinburgh.

In the end it was not the walls that failed but Rome itself. Time and again frontier troops were pulled out to support attempts by upstart generalissimos who yearned to be emperor. Weaknesses from within caused Rome to fall, as well as pressures from without; the same drive to power that created the empire eventually tore it apart.

By the year 410, Rome had been sacked by the Gauls. In that same year the emperor Honorius informed his commanders in Britain that they were now on their own.

Yet the impact of Rome endures in Britain, in the high place the Classics have always held in British education, but most clearly in the English language itself. Well over sixty percent of the words in English derive from Latin. In the very words I write, in the very words you speak, the voice of Rome still rings.

17

Human Sacrifice in Denmark

Bodies in the Bog

THEY STOOD in the churchyard at Elsinore: two gravediggers with their tools and, at a distance in the fog, Hamlet, prince of Denmark. The grave was to be beloved Ophelia's, who had died by drowning.

Hamlet approached one of the diggers and asked, "How long will a man lie i' the earth ere he rot?"

"Eight or nine years" was the reply. "But a tanner will last nine."

"Why he more than another?" asked Hamlet.

"Because," the gravedigger answered, "his hide is so tanned with his trade that he will keep out water a great while."

Then, still digging, the workmen uncovered Yorick's skull.[45]

*   *   *   *

The telephone rang a hundred miles west of Elsinore. It was the police calling Professor P. V. Glob at Aarhus University. The year was 1950, and a body had just been uncovered by two peat cutters at a bog called Tollund Fen *(Thor's Grave)*. Fearing foul play, the peat cutters had called the police, but

The preserved head of the Tollund Man.

the police—suspecting the corpse was ancient—had in turn called upon Dr. Glob, a professor of European archaeology.

Some two hundred square miles of Denmark are covered by deposits of peat. Peat consists of compressed vegetable matter from dead mosses. For thousands of years men in Europe have used peat moss as a fuel for heating and cooking. As the moss decays in the bog, an acid—akin to the tannic acid used to "tan" leather—is released into the surrounding water. This acid and its preservative powers accounted for the survival of the body Dr. Glob would soon inspect.

As he looked down the seven-foot vertical face of umber brown peat, he saw—lying on the floor of the cutting—the figure of a man asleep, resting on his right side, his arms and legs bent back, his eyes gently closed. The figure was naked except for the smooth hide belt around his waist and the pointed leather cap tied with two thin thongs beneath his chin.

As Professor Glob climbed down into the pit and looked at the corpse more closely, he was fascinated by the well-preserved condition of the man's skin. It had been stained to the same brown hue as the peat that had enclosed it. The skin pores were clearly visible on the clean-shaven face which still bore a short stubble on its surface. Beneath the wrinkled brow, eyebrows arched over closed eyes. The cheeks were high and full, the nose curved, the lips pursed. Elsewhere on the naked body, however, the skin hung in folds and bones frequently protruded.

The grimmest evidence emerged when a piece of peat next to the head was removed. Beneath it, a twisted leather-thong rope could be seen knotted behind the neck and still pulled tight around the throat. The rest of the rope, five-feet long and cut off at the end, trailed over the shoulder and down the back. The *Tollund Man* had died by hanging. His killers had chosen the peat bog as the place to dispose of the body. But the depth of his corpse beneath the decomposing moss showed that execution had taken place in antiquity.

The bog was to claim yet another victim. Now that the body was exposed to air, it had to be removed from the site and protected before further decomposition set in. A one-ton section of peat containing the corpse was cut away and crated, but as it was being lifted manually ten feet up from the pit, one of the workers engaged in the hoisting operation suffered a heart attack and died.

After this incident the body of the Tollund Man was taken to the laboratory of the National Museum in Copen-hagen where it was examined by scientific experts. X-ray studies revealed the presence of a brain, albeit shrunken, still in the skull; images of wisdom teeth showed the victim had been at least twenty when he died. Interesting results also came from an inspection of the corpse's alimentary canal. The Tollund Man had eaten his last meal between twelve and twenty-four hours prior to his death. The material taken from his intestines revealed no evidence of meat, only a mixture of grain and seeds from wild plants. When the ancient recipe was reproduced later for a special BBC pro-gram, an archaeologist sampling the gruel commented that eating it on a regular basis would have been punishment enough for the Tollund Man; hanging would have been superfluous!

It was soon realized by the museum that preserving the whole body would be too difficult; the head, however, could be saved. The head, newly severed from the body, was soaked by technicians for months in a series of solutions (water, formalin, and acetic acid; alcohol; alcohol and toluol; and pure toluol) and saturated in warm parafin and wax so that it could be put on display—the "best preserved head from antiquity in any part of the world."[46] Alas! Poor Yorick.

Two years later, in the spring, a second body was uncov-ered in a bog just a few miles from Tollund near the village of Grauballe. This time the peat cutters informed the village doctor, who called Professor Glob to the scene.

The *Grauballe Man,* as he came to be called, lay on his chest, his head twisted to one side and compressed by the weight of peat it had borne. Tufts of dark hair, turned red-dish by acid, still clung to the dark-brown scalp. The ribs, visible through the flattened back, and the loose folds of skin made the body seem like a melting plastic manikin. Eyeballs and fingernails, however, were still intact.

Transported to a special laboratory at Aarhus University, the body was carefully examined. Evidence of incipient rheumatoid arthritis of the spine suggested that the Grauballe Man had been at least thirty years old. His teeth showed heavy wear and bore holes and signs of abscess. In his stomach were found the remains of his last meal, eaten shortly before death: again a gruel, this time made up of over sixty different types of grains and wild seeds including spelt rye, rye-grass, clover, Yorkshire fog, goosefoot, buttercup, lady's mantle, black nightshade, yarrow, smooth hawksbeard, and wild camomile.

No elaborate examination was needed to determine the cause of his death: his throat had been slashed from ear to ear, and the character of the wound indicated it was not self-inflicted. A skull fracture on the upper temple caused by a blow from a blunt instrument suggested he had first been knocked unconscious. Like the Tollund Man, he had died violently and had been deposited, naked, in a bog by his killers.

The skin on his hands and on the soles of his feet were so remarkably preserved that members of the Aarhus police were able to take his footprints and fingerprints and proclaim them sharp enough for criminal identification purposes. The condition of his hands, moreover, indicated that the Grauballe Man had not done rough work during his life.

To determine when his death had occurred, the peat in which he was enveloped was analyzed for pollen. By discovering what plants were growing around the bog when he died (based on the microscopic pollen grains preserved in the peat), palaeobotanists were able to deduce that the Grauballe Man lived during the first four centuries of the Christian era. This dating was confirmed by measurements of the radioactive carbon content of his liver and muscle tissue. The degree to which the radioactivity in his body had degenerated—from the constant level it would have had while he was alive—pointed to his death as having occurred between A.D. 210 and 410, the period in Danish archaeological history known as the late Roman Iron Age, the time during which the Tollund Man also had probably lived.

Scholars at the Museum of Prehistory at Aarhus wanted to try to preserve not just the head but the Grauballe Man's entire body. To do so they decided to intensify artificially the tanning process that had been taking place naturally in the bog and, for expert advice, turned to none other than the Danish Guild of Tanners. The method used —pit tanning—took a little over a year and a half to complete and required the use of almost two thousand pounds of oak bark. Following the tanning, the corpse was bathed for a month in Turkish red oil and distilled water, air-dried, and then impregnated with glycerin, lanolin, and cod-liver oil, after which the body parts that had best retained their shape were injected with collodion. The method worked and succeeded in preserving the body of an ancient Dane two thousand years old.

Although they are the most famous and most carefully examined, the Tollund and Grauballe men are not the only bodies from the past to have been found in bogs. In Denmark alone, over one hundred fifty have been discovered during the last two centuries, and almost six hundred more have been found in other countries of Western Europe, especially Germany. Most seem to date between 100 B.C. and A.D. 500 and probably represent only a fraction of the bodies the bogs must still hold. Almost all show evidence of having died violently. Some were hanged like the Tollund Man or had their throats cut like the Grauballe Man; others were decapitated, strangled, or drowned. They include men, women, and children, deposited with no grave furnishings and most often naked, sometimes with sticks or stones placed over their bodies like weights to hold them down. Denmark's *Borre Fen Man* still wears on his twisted face a look of terror.

The Roman historian Tacitus, describing the customs of Germanic tribes in the first-century A.D., tells of criminals being hanged or thrown in bogs.[47] But Professor Glob believes the bodies in Denmark and perhaps elsewhere may reflect another custom: the making of human sacrifices to the goddess of earth and fertility. He notes the special nature of the condemned man's "last meal"—a special and probably ceremonial meal composed of as many types of seeds as could be found, a symbolic meal representing the hoped-for springtime rebirth of vegetative life. He points to the absence of seeds from berries or apples as an indication that the ceremony must have taken place during the dark and cold days of winter, which people of the Iron Age feared might not end unless the Earth Mother were propitiated. Even the noose around the necks of some victims may echo the double choker necklace worn by the Earth Mother in art. So perished the ancient ancestors of Hamlet and Ophelia.

Of all the bog bodies that have been found, one of the most poignant is that of a young girl found in 1952 in Domland Fen. Before she was drowned, her red, yellow, and brown headband had been placed as a blindfold over her eyes. The hair had been shaved from the left side of her head, a likely punishment for adultery. When her body was found, the colorful blindfold still held taut around her face as she slept on the bed of peat.

> Her clothes spread wide,
> And, mermaid-like, awhile they bore her up;
> Which time she chanted snatches of old tunes,
> As one incapable of her own distress,
> Or like a creature native and indued
> Unto that element; but long it could not be
> Till that her garments, heavy with their drink,
> Pull'd the poor wretch from her melodious lay
> To muddy death.[48]

18

King Arthur and History

The Quest for Camelot

Each evening from December to December
Before you drift to sleep upon your cot,
Think back on all the tales that you remember
Of Camelot.

Ask ev'ry person if he's heard the story;
And tell it strong and clear if he has not;
That once there was a fleeting wisp of glory
Called Camelot.

Where once it never rained till after sundown;
By eight a.m. the morning fog had flown . . .
Don't let it be forgot
That once there was a spot
For one brief shining moment that was known
As Camelot . . . [49]

THESE WORDS, and the music that springs from them
in Lerner and Loewe's *Camelot,* are sung by a king who never
died—the legendary Arthur, human symbol of chivalry's
highest ideals.

Inspired by T. H. White's novel, *The Once and Future King,*
the stage and screen versions of *Camelot* echo still earlier

Gustave Doré's vision of Camelot.

literary accounts of Arthur, Queen Guinevere, and brave Lancelot: Lord Tennyson's nineteenth-century *Idylls of the King* and Sir Thomas Malory's fifteenth-century *Le Morte d'Artur*.

These in turn can be traced to an anonymous 13th century French romance, *La Mort le Roi Artu (The Death of King Arthur)*. In fact, so popular was the story of Arthur in thirteenth-century France that a poet and Crusader named Jean Bodel of Arras said there were only three subjects worth writing about: the matter of the ancient world (Greece and Rome); the matter of France (Charlemagne and French knighthood); and what he termed the "matter of Britain" (the stories of Arthur and the knights of the Round Table).

Although in our imagination we may associate King Arthur with the full flowering of the Middle Ages, he really belonged to an earlier time. Arthur's name appears in twelfth-century French, Italian, and German tales of chivalry (as does the name Camelot). Arthur is depicted in an inscribed mosaic and a captioned stone relief from eleventh-century Italy, and his valor and death are described in tenth-century literature. In an eighth-century work, he is spoken of as "Artorius." Indeed, Arthur appears in literature as early as the sixth century, where his bravery is described and he is called "the Bear" (*arth* or *artos* in Celtic).

The date of these sources would place Arthur not in the Middle Ages but rather in the earlier Dark Ages, when the Empire of Rome had fallen and barbarian hordes swept across Europe. When Rome let go its hold on Britain, Saxons from the continent invaded. It is against them that Arthur would have fought as leader of the Britons sometime around A.D. 500.

Yet difficulties surround the search for a physical confirmation of Arthur's birth and death. Although tradition says Arthur was conceived at Tintagel Castle, a dramatic cliffside site on the Cornish coast, the oldest castle there dates back only to the twelfth century; before that time Tintagel was the site of a Celtic monastery.

Concerning Arthur's death and burial, we are told that he was borne by barge to the isle of Avalon after being mortally wounded in battle. There his body was given burial. In fact, medieval tradition points to the very site of his burial.

This tradition states that in the days of Richard the Lionhearted, the grave of Arthur and Queen Guinevere was discovered at Glastonbury Abbey in southwest England. Glastonbury was revered as the site of the first Christian church established on English soil. Here, in 1195, the monks of the abbey uncovered a grave. In the grave were the skeletons of a man and a woman. The bones of the man were enormous; on the skull of the woman a lock of yellow hair still clung. Nearby a lead cross lay whose inscription read: "Here lies buried the renowned King Arthur in the isle of Avalon." A second version adds the words "with Guinevere his second wife."

Skeptics point out that the abbey had burned down some years before and that the "discovery" may have been faked by the monks to attract pilgrims and generate contributions for the abbey's rebuilding. Politically, the "discovery" may have also been devised to squelch—by the evidence of Arthur's own bones—the rumors that Arthur had been reborn in the person of Arthur of Brittany, then a claimant to the English throne. Moreover, an extant drawing of the lead cross suggests a style of lettering only tenth or eleventh century in date, although it has been argued that such a cross—later in date—may have been added to Arthur's original grave site.

In any event, the cross was last seen in the eighteenth century and its whereabouts are now unknown. The grave itself was reopened in the thirteenth century by King Edward I, who transferred the bones to a special tomb in front of Glastonbury's altar, but in the days of Henry VIII the tomb was violated and the bones thereafter vanished.

Although the authenticity of this site has been disputed, the holiness of Glastonbury and the fact that it was once an island in a marsh support the argument that it is the legendary Avalon where Arthur was laid to rest.

Yet what of Camelot, the legendary base of Arthur's power and the site of his castle? Even though a number of sites in England bear ruins of early fortresses, none is so imposing as those at Cadbury in Somerset, not far from Glastonbury. Cadbury "Castle," as it is known, had been identified as the site of Arthur's Camelot as far back as 1532 by one John Leland, who found etymological confirmation in the presence of the nearby river Camel.

In 1966 the specially created Camelot Research Committee began excavating the site to determine if it was in fact used as a fortress during the days of Arthur at the time of the Saxon invasion of England.

Surrounded by pastureland and ringed by a forest, the mound of Cadbury rises two hundred fifty feet to a summit that spreads over eighteen acres. Adjoining the surrounding trees were found the remains of four concentric ramparts and ditches. On the summit itself, the archaeologists, led by Leslie Alcock, found traces in the soil of postholes and foundations of an impressive complex of structures. Within wooden fortress walls, fitted with watchtower and gateway, had been two wells, storehouses, and stables that could accommodate a sizable cavalry force. Most impressive of all were the foundations of a great feasting hall, gabled at each end and measuring thirty by sixty feet. If there ever was a Round Table, this would have been its site.

Sifting the soil, the archaeological team also found pottery sherds, fragments of jewelry, some coins, and rusting bits of iron weaponry. The age of the pottery and coins showed the fortress had been built about A.D. 470 and had continued in use into the sixth century as the most powerfully fortified site in Dark Age England. This then would have been Camelot.

The humble remains, muted by the centuries that buried them, seem so out of accord with the bright banners we see flying over the spires of the Camelot of our imagination. Some would even say that rather than proving the existence of Arthur the paltry physical evidence reduces his stature to less than heroic size. But we would be remiss to think that valor and dreams can ever be measured in a handful of potsherds or in bits of rusting armor. As long as the human spirit longs for a better world, Camelot and Arthur will live on—an untarnished dream without which we would all be the poorer.

It was Sir Winston Churchill, leader of England during a modern-day battle for Britain, who put it best. Surveying the evidence *pro* and *con* for Arthur's existence, Sir Winston concluded:

> Let us declare that King Arthur and his noble knights set decent folk an example for all time. It is all true, or it ought to be; and more and better besides.[50]

19

England's Oldest Royal Grave

The Treasure of Sutton Hoo

AS WORLD WAR II searchlights scanned the night sky, as the bombs of the German attack burst upon London, painting the canvas of night with the orange-red glow of buildings ablaze, a small group of wooden crates sat huddled in the dark stillness of a deserted subway tunnel. Deep beneath the siren's wail and the clanging of fire bells, the boxes stood secure from the war that raged above. They had been put there for safety by the staff of the British Museum, for carefully packed inside them were the weapons and regalia of an ancient English king, "the most marvellous find in the archaeological annals of England,"[51] "the richest treasure ever dug from British soil."[52]

*   *   *   *

The story begins in the summer of 1938, shortly before the outbreak of war, some seventy miles northeast of London, on a country estate owned by Mrs. Edith May Pretty. There beside the River Deben a promontory, or *hoo*, called *Sutton Hoo* overlooked the sea.

For as long as she had gazed out her drawing-room win-

The royal helmet from Sutton Hoo after its reconstruction.

dow, Mrs. Pretty had been curious about the low mounds that dotted her property. They were barrows, or ancient burial mounds, and tradition said they contained buried treasure. Finally deciding to satisfy her curiosity, she invited the local Ipswich Museum to explore them. The archaeologist from the museum, Mr. Basil Brown, was given temporary quarters in Mrs. Pretty's house and was entrusted with a staff of two gardeners to help him. This would serve as a humble beginning for what would turn out to be a remarkable story of discovery.

Basil Brown's initial finds were predictable and not especially exciting: some human bones and some simple objects, rusted or corroded, that had been placed with the dead. The graves had apparently been robbed centuries before, the most recent "excavators" being rabbits who had burrowed into the mounds to make their homes.

Brown continued, however, and directed his attention to the largest of the barrows on the estate, a mound approximately one hundred feet long, some seventy-five feet wide, and nine feet high.

Brown decided to slice a trench down through the middle of the mound. As the earth and sand below it was removed, an amazing image began slowly to appear. Out of the densely packed sand emerged the outline of a ship's keel. Although the original timbers had rotted away, the sand had preserved an impression of the boat's shape. Rusty iron rivets that had once held the timbers together were still embedded in the sand in their original positions. As the center of the boat was cleared, artifacts began to appear. Brown realized that he had come upon something unusual indeed, and called upon the British Museum in London for expert assistance.

During Europe's Dark Ages, it had been the custom for some peoples, such as the Vikings, to bury their seafaring chieftains in ships to provide for their final journey to Valhalla. Such burials had actually been discovered during the nineteenth century in Scandinavia. The most famous were found in Norway.

In 1880 a seventy-nine-foot-long Viking ship was

unearthed in Gokstad. Dated to the ninth century A.D., it contained the remains of a fifty-year-old man accompanied by twelve horses, six dogs, furniture, and a peacock. In 1903 at Oseberg (also in Norway) another Viking ship, sixty-nine feet long, was found with the remains of a woman—likely a queen—and the remains of a slave buried with her to serve her needs in the afterlife. The wood of both ships, beautifully carved, was miraculously preserved: the graves had been dug in a blue clay that held each boat in a watertight "bottle" for a thousand years.

Both Viking ships can be seen today in their museum home in Oslo. That the ships are seaworthy was demonstrated in 1892, the four hundredth anniversary of Columbus's "discovery" of America, when a crew of patriotic Norwegians—to bolster claims that the Vikings had been first—made a successful trans-Atlantic voyage in a scale model of the Gokstad ship.

Even though the wood of the Sutton Hoo ship had not survived, a determination of its size could be made from the impressions left in the sand. It was eighty-nine feet long, longer than either Viking boat. No evidence of mast or deck was found: Rather it was like a huge open rowboat, manned by a crew of some forty oarsmen with a great steering oar at the stern. When archaeologists later made a cast of the boat, six and a half tons of plaster were required.

Not only was the Sutton Hoo ship larger than the Viking craft that had been found, it was also older by some two centuries, as determined by inscriptions found on its cargo. Dated to the seventh century A.D., it stands as "the first known English war-vessel."[53]

After the epics of ancient Greece and Rome, the oldest heroic poem in Western literature is *Beowulf*, composed in England only a century after the Sutton Hoo ship sailed the seas. Beowulf, hero of the poem, is buried with his treasure on a headland, or *hoo*, overlooking the sea after his dragon-slaying days are over.[54] Elsewhere, the epic describes a funeral at sea using a treasure-laden death ship.[55] Taken together, the two passages reflect the ritual and ceremony that infused the burial at Sutton Hoo. Viewed from the opposite perspective, the discovery at Sutton Hoo serves to illustrate the very substance of England's oldest epic.

* * * *

As the excavation proceeded, under the leadership of C. W. Phillips, the Sutton Hoo ship yielded its precious cargo of gold, silver, and gems. Yet two ceremonial objects, not of silver or gold, were to become crucially important in assessing the significance of the discovery. An elaborate iron standard, almost six feet tall, and a six-pound whetstone carved with eight austere faces indicated to scholars that they had come upon the burial of no simple chieftain but a king. The treasure they would unearth would be the regalia of an Anglo-Saxon king, "the richest single archaeological discovery ever made in the British Isles."[56]

The monarch had been buried with his sword and shield as befitted a warrior. The sword had a blade twenty-eight inches long; its pommel was jeweled and its scabbard adorned with gold. Only the metal boss and handle fittings of the shield survived, but from where they lay it could be seen that the shield had had a three-foot diameter. Golden buckles and clasps from the king's leathern battle gear and rusting iron chain mail also survived. The gold of his royal equipment had been intricately fashioned into elaborate abstract cloisonné patterns that were inset with over four thousand individually cut garnets.

Just as extraordinary was the warrior's helmet. Oversized like a crash helmet and very probably padded, it provided armored protection to the head, full face, and back of the neck. It had been made of iron overlaid with tinned bronze upon which the metalsmith had hammered out warriors and battle scenes on plaques. The king had heavy eyebrows and a short mustache that were reproduced in metal. To make his face look fearsome, his eyebrows were made to end with gilded boars' heads, while a silver ridge made of garnet-eyed dragons climbed from his nose to the crown of his head. All these raised metallic parts had a physical as well as a psychological function: They could take and absorb the blows of an enemy sword.

In the afterlife, as in life itself, after battle came feasting, and the king was amply outfitted for both. No less than seven drinking horns were found, two of them with six-quart capacities. Because they were horns, incidentally, they could not be set down: they would have to be passed around or guzzled at one sitting. Imported (plundered?) silver bowls —one with a refined late-Classical head tooled inside, another bearing the stamp of a fifth-century Byzantine emperor—were also included.

For entertainment a six-stringed lyre was provided, made of maplewood and oak and stored in a beaver-skin sack. Protected by a bowl, its upper part escaped being eaten away by acid soil; the sounding box—outside—succumbed. An ivory token (the others must have disintegrated) revealed the onetime presence of a game, while traces of goose-down feathers showed a pillow had also been packed for the king's comfort.

One of the most historically valuable and at the same time curious discoveries was a gold and garnet cloisonné purse that held thirty-seven gold coins, three coin-sized gold blanks, and two small gold ingots. Most of the coins had legible designs and inscriptions that allowed the archaeologists not only to identify the provenance and age of the coins but also to assign an approximate date to the ship burial. All the coins were Merovingian French (from France, Belgium, Switzerland, or the Rhineland), each from a different mint, and none had been minted later than A.D. 625 or 630, so the funeral must have taken place after that time.

But why was this group of coins part of the cargo? The intrinsic value of the gold was not so great as to make this a royal treasure. Had the English king been a coin collector who wished to take his hobby with him to the next world? The real explanation may lie in the number of gold pieces on board: the thirty-seven coins and three blanks could have been intended as pay for the forty ghostly oarsmen who would row the king to the beyond; the extra gold ingots, special pay for the helmsman manning the great steering oar.

But had the royal passenger ever gotten on board? No skeleton was found, not even part of a skeleton, although the acidity of the sand might explain the disappearance of a body. Traces of cremated bone were found near a dish, but they may indicate an animal sacrifice or funeral feast. High levels of bone phosphates along the keel-line between helmet and sword are intriguing evidence, but not proof positive that the king's body once lay there.

Had the king been lost at sea like King Aethelwald and been given a funeral in absentia? Had he been converted to Christianity like King Anna (missionaries had only recently come to England) and been buried in the sanctified ground of a churchyard? Twin silver spoons, inscribed "Saul" and "Paul" in Greek, were found in the boat and may have been used at the king's christening. But why then the ship burial, a pagan rite? Perhaps the king had hedged his bets, agreeing to have his body buried in a churchyard but ordering a heroic funeral in accordance with ancestral custom as well. If so, he might have been King Raedwald; it is said he worshiped Christ and Woden side by side. Aethelwald, Anna, Raedwald—all recorded as seventh-century kings of the Angles and each a possible name on the ghost ship's passenger list.

Apart from not finding a body, the archaeologists had been extraordinarily lucky. In the dirt above the treasure they found the remains of a campfire and a jug from Shakespeare's day. Elizabethan grave robbers had apparently dug down into the barrow but, not finding anything, gave up and picnicked instead—all the time only ten feet above where the treasure lay!

But the luck the archaeological team experienced was coupled with urgency: many of the materials that emerged from the sand (bits of leather and wood) were organic; freed of their moist environment, they would rapidly disintegrate unless they were prevented from drying out. Other objects were of perishable metal (rusting iron or corroding bronze) and required emergency treatment to keep fresh air from hastening the oxidation process. The crushed and fragmentary state of some of the finds presented special problems: the helmet, for example, had decayed into as many as four hundred separate fragments. Also, much of the treasure, like the helmet, had been crushed by the collapse of an ancient roof built over the boat's center.

The unique character of the Sutton Hoo discovery meant there was no "rule book" on how to excavate and preserve, and the materials themselves did not allow time for such a rule book to be written. And, given that almost no Anglo-Saxon sites had ever before been dug, there were no experts to turn to and there was no time to call upon colleagues from the continent. Dedicated improvisation was the order of the day, as materials were damp-packed in moss for express transport back to the laboratories of the British Museum, where a battle would be waged to preserve the objects for later study.

Meanwhile, another kind of battle threatened: as the excavation proceeded, the clouds of a second world war were growing darker by the hour, adding pressure to the urgency the diggers already felt. On September 1, 1939—only six days after the digging ended—World War II began.

Just two weeks earlier a strange episode had occurred in the story of Sutton Hoo: a coroner's inquest was held to determine who owned the boat and its cargo. According to English law, all buried treasure that is found is Crown property, provided the treasure was buried in secret and was meant to be recovered later. If these conditions are not met, the treasure becomes the property of the landowner. And so in the spirit of English democracy a local jury was convened to decide the issue. After due deliberation, the coroner's jury decided that the treasure was neither buried in secret (the ancient funeral had been public) nor was it ever meant to be reclaimed (it was to be the king's forever). Hence, they ruled, Mrs. Edith May Pretty, owner of the land on which the treasure had been found, was its rightful owner. Thus the disposition of a king's treasure, the most ancient royal treasure ever found on English soil, was decided by a jury that included a retired military officer, a farmer, a bank manager, a tax collector, a golf-club secretary, a haulage contractor, a village grocer, a real-estate agent, a blacksmith, and a schoolteacher.

A little over a week later an even more remarkable announcement was made. In an act of selfless patriotism, Mrs. Pretty stated that she was making a gift of the treasure to the nation, one of the most generous private bequests in the history of archaeology.

Under threat of impending aerial bombardment, the treasure of Sutton Hoo—carefully packed and crated—was stored by British Museum staff members in an unused tunnel beneath London's streets. There the last remains of an ancient English warrior would rest safe from weapons he could never have understood.

20

The Tomb of China's First Emperor

Inside the Great Wall

DEEP WITHIN the red earthen mound, in a chamber sealed by a jade door, his body rests in a copper coffin. Nearby in the darkness stands a model of the universe. Beneath the jeweled stars of its dome, twin rivers of mercury flow silently into a quicksilver sea. Automatic crossbows are aimed and set, as they have been for twenty-two centuries, waiting for those who would violate the emperor's tomb.

His name was Ying Cheng, and he was warlord at the age of thirteen. But that was not enough; it would never be enough. For twenty-five years he battled against the other warlords of his land until he had defeated them all, marching against them with a million armored soldiers, ten thousand horses, and a thousand chariots until he had devoured his enemies "as the silkworm devours the mulberry leaf." He slaughtered forty thousand soldiers in a single campaign (*after* they had surrendered) and upon victory ordered colossal statues of himself made from the melted metal of all his enemies' weapons.

To do justice to his omnipotence he needed a new title, and it was instantly created: *Huang Ti*, Divine Emperor. Born

Life-size terra-cotta soldier found beside the tomb of China's first emperor.

in the province of Ch'in, and first member *(Shih)* of a dynasty he boasted would last ten thousand years, his full title would become *Ch'in Shih Huang Ti,* First Divine Emperor of China, by the force of his personality giving to the land the name we call it by today.

The emperor was determined to make his power endure. Dismantling the old feudal system, he established a strong centralized monarchy, unifying the separate provinces of his country into a cohesive nation administered under a uniform code of law. To connect the distant parts of his realm, he ordered the construction of a great system of roads and canals. Irrigation projects increased agricultural productivity. Writing was standardized throughout the land to make communication easier, and weights and measures were made standard to facilitate commerce. Because of these progressive steps, Emperor Ch'in was to become a hero to China's twentieth-century leader, Mao Tse Tung, who admired the emperor because he had fought aristocratic claims to land and lordship and had fathered the modern Chinese state.

Yet, just as Mao's own Great Leap Forward was ruthless, so were the reforms of Emperor Ch'in. Many Confucian scholars, considered politically dangerous because of their beliefs, were sent to forced labor camps just as in the days of Mao's Red Guard when professors were physically abused. Book burning also took place as a means of thought control, especially in the case of philosophical works deemed critical of Ch'in's regime. And to finance one man's dream, heavy taxation fell upon all.

The seat of the empire was a magnificent new capital city, near the modern city of Xian *(shee an)* in the Wei River Valley of Shaanxi Province. The city was laid out in accordance with a cosmic plan of design and the scope of construction was vast. The main palace alone measured a mile and a half long and a half-mile wide, with thousands of rooms and an audience hall that could hold ten thousand subjects. But the main palace was joined to two hundred seventy more, interconnected by covered passageways and built so the emperor could avoid assassination by sleeping in a different palace each night. It was said that when the city eventually caught fire, it burned for three months.

The emperor's most enduring monument was intended as a line of defense to keep raiders from the barbaric north out of his domain. But as a line of demarcation it served another function: it defined the new nation physically. We know this monument as the Great Wall of China.

The third century B.C. Great Wall is actually a series of older feudal walls linked together by new construction into a continuous line of protection. It took ten years to build and was erected by the forced labor of prisoners of war and Confucian convicts. We are told that during the course of its construction tens of thousands died. If we are to believe ancient tradition, their bones were ground up and added to the mortar, making the Wall the "longest cemetery on earth."

Long it is, spanning fifteen hundred miles from the Pacific Ocean to the Gobi Desert—double that length and more if we stretch taut its dragonlike twists and turns, as far as a journey from Los Angeles to New York and back again to Chicago. Reaching over one-twentieth of the earth's circumference, it is one of the longest marks left by the hand of man on this planet. Surmounted by a twenty-foot-high roadway wide enough for eight men marching abreast, it connects a total of twenty-five-thousand forty-foot-high watchtowers set two bow shots apart to provide complete ballistic coverage. Messages in smoke or fire transmitted along these towers could cross ancient China in twenty-four hours or less. Among the aged graffiti scratched on the wall is one possessing striking modernity: "Beware the Russians!"

The planning that went into the building of the Great Wall is matched only by the effort the emperor expended to construct his final resting place. Tradition tells us that seventy thousand conscripts worked on the project and that it took more than a decade to complete.

The emperor's tomb was a pyramid-shaped earthen hill representing, in cosmic imagery, the zenith of heaven. Over a quarter of a mile on each side of its square base, it rose in three tiers to a total height of fifteen stories. Surrounding it were two walls, constituting a spiritual "city" with temples and other monuments. A history written a century later tells us that inside the tomb were placed "models of palaces, towers, and official buildings, as well as fine utensils, precious stones, and rarities." These objects included an ingenious model of the emperor's earthly empire with the Yellow and Yang-tze rivers in mercury flowing by mechanical means into a mercury ocean beneath a jeweled sky. To ensure security, the artisans who knew the tomb's secrets were afterward executed.

The secrets of the emperor's tomb were kept until 1932, when the first of a series of five kneeling figures in terracotta were found by peasants ploughing in the fields surrounding the artificial hill. Then, in March 1974, peasants digging a well made a startling discovery. Buried in the earth were large human figures of baked clay, bigger than life-size, between 5'8" and 6'2" tall, the largest sculptured figures that have ever been found in the history of Chinese art. The figures were of soldiers buried in anticipation of the emperor's death to serve as his eternal bodyguards in the spirit world. For as he had deserved such an entourage in life, so did he deserve to have one in death.

But soon scientific excavations revealed the full dimensions of the farmers' initial discovery. These were not merely a few bodyguards but an entire army! Slowly, carefully, the bodies of hundreds upon hundreds of pottery soldiers rose and stood at attention—a total of six thousand infantry soldiers, horses, and attendants, precisely arranged in military formation on the bricked floor of an underground chamber two hundred feet wide by seven hundred feet long.

This had been a very colorful army indeed. Traces of pigment still clung to the clay. One contingent wore green tunics with collars and cuffs of purple and trousers of blue; a second was dressed in red tunics with blue collars and cuffs and trousers in blue and green. Their armored (leather?) vests were painted in black or brown, tied with purple or orange thongs, riveted in white, red, and green, and buckled in golden yellow. Their shoes were uniformly black, but laced in bright orange.

The skin of the warriors was painted not yellow but pink. Their hair and eyebrows were black, and each soldier wore a mustache and small pointed beard. Within the whites of their eyes were black painted irises.

The detail that had been incised into the still-soft clay revealed painstaking execution, from the hobnailed soles of the shoes to the sharply etched strands of the chignoned hair.

Most extraordinary are the faces: each individualized and no two alike among the thousands we can inspect. Each is the portrait of a particular soldier who served in the emperor's actual army, an artistic approach that may have been intended to guarantee for these troops a shared immortality with their sovereign in the world beyond.

Each head was made of solid clay set upon a hollow torso that stood on solid legs. Constructing and operating the huge kilns needed to bake these thousands of soldiers would in itself have been a mighty feat of engineering.

The troops stand four abreast in nine columns over six hundred fifty feet long. At the formation's rear and along each side stand alert guardians facing outward. At the van is the unit's firepower: two hundred archers and kneeling warriors with crossbows poised to fire at an unseen enemy ahead. Near the front are six chariots, two of them commanding vehicles. Each chariot is drawn by four lively and life-size clay horses with white teeth and hooves and red nostrils. Even though the wood of the chariots has long since disintegrated, their frames and spoked wheels remain impressed in the earth.

In addition to the infantry and chariots, thousands of weapon parts have been found, including metal arrowheads and crossbow triggers, but the empty hands of most warriors and the carbonized remains of the wood superstructure that housed them suggest that the "barracks," never very deep beneath the ground, had been pillaged in ancient times and burnt.

In May 1976, a second pit was discovered filled mostly with cavalry soldiers and war chariots, and the next month a headquarters pit was found containing imposing statues of commanding officers. It is estimated that decades may pass before these pits are entirely excavated. A fourth pit, found completely empty, indicates that the grandiose project of burying an entire pottery army was abandoned, probably because of the emperor's death.

He did indeed die in 210 B.C., although he had wished to live forever. Tradition tells us he commanded his wise men to find him, on pain of death, the Fountain of Youth. Although he had boasted his dynasty would last ten thousand years, it ended after fourteen, the shortest dynasty in Chinese history. Victim of a plot by his prime minister and chief eunuch, he died at the age of forty-nine.

To buy time, the conspirators maintained the fiction that he was still alive, bringing his body back from the northern provinces in a closed carriage, which they occasionally approached as though to deliver meals or receive orders. When the rotting body began to smell (it was summer), a cart of salted fish was brought up to obscure the odor. Thus the Divine Emperor of China made his final journey home leading a fish cart.

To eliminate the emperor's rightful heir, his eldest son, the conspirators forged a letter in his father's name bidding him to commit suicide which, in his obedience, he did. A forged will then made the conspirators' candidate, Ch'in's second son, monarch.

Archaeologists have found evidence of the aftermath of the assassination. Near the emperor's own funeral mound, smaller "satellite" tombs have been found. The close ages of the occupants, all between twenty and thirty years old as determined by skeletal remains, suggest they were princely age-mates who died at the same time. Along with royal seals that bore their names and funeral objects that filled their coffins, signs were found that explain their end. Some skeletons bear marks of mutilation: some of their body parts were buried *outside* their coffins. Some have dislocated jaws—an indication of hanging. Others have bronze arrowheads still embedded in their skulls behind the ear. All had died violently, murdered to ensure a smooth succession.

Eventually, the prime minister would die the "death of a thousand cuts": his slashed body, minus nose, feet, and genitalia, would be cut in two at the waist; the chief eunuch would commit suicide; and the ambitious second son would be murdered by an even more ambitious nephew.

*   *   *   *

Today, beneath a metallic structure that resembles an airplane hangar, the loyal troops of Emperor Ch'in still stand at attention. A mile away, fruit trees grow on his funeral mound. Its entrance has never been found; its interior never explored by archaeologists.

Perhaps the strings of the automatic crossbows hidden inside have long since rotted away. Perhaps the copper coffin has corroded, green beyond recognition. Or perhaps somewhere in the still darkness, jeweled stars are waiting to sparkle once again, and rivers of quicksilver to shimmer once more as they course to an endless sea.

21

The Mystery of Easter Island

The Fallen Idols

THEIR LITTLE BOATS bobbed up and down on the rolling expanse of the Pacific. Current and wind had borne them now a thousand miles and more from land. With them traveled stores of fresh water, chickens in wicker cages, and sweet potatoes for planting in the new homeland their chief had told them they would somehow find.

Who was the first to see, scanning the horizon for weeks, the island rising out of the sea—Rapa Nui—most remote of all Polynesian isles, a small triangle of mountainous green?

Here was no paradise, but it was still a place to stop, to end the empty eternity of seeking a new home, a promised home that had never seemed to come. The breakers smashed against the eight-hundred-foot cliffs, the wind swept the volcanic terrain, but here they could plant their taro and yams, scatter seed to their livestock, and live.

Their chief—the memory of his shameful defeat behind him—would rule them until he died. Then his twelve children, each taking part of the island for a realm, would rule them in his stead.

*   *   *   *

A thousand years would pass before a great surge of religion lifted them all in its swell. First, along the island's perimeter,

Stone statue from Easter Island.

they erected ramped platforms of stone *(ahu)*, poised at the edge of the sea from which they had come. Then later they mounted the volcanic slopes in search of stone and quarried huge blocks *(moai)*, hewn with human features. Two and three times a man's height were the stones, twenty to ninety tons each. Down from the rocky slopes in gangs they dragged them, hauling them to their platformed sites. With ropes and levers, propping them with rocks, they tilted them upright upon the altars. Some statues they set in long ranks to gaze in unison across the landscape of the faithful. These were the potent ancestors, the ones great with magic. These were the gods. In time three hundred stood.

From jutting brows, long, big-nostriled noses descended to downturned lips. Long ears drooped with heavy earplugs. Rigid arms pressed against the sides of torsos from which protuberant bellies but no legs emerged. The eyes were hollow, deep, ever-brooding. On the haughty heads sat ten-ton capstones of red volcanic rock.

Some say these were the bodies and faces of the "heavyset ones," the *Hanau Eepe*, who had come as a second wave from across the sea and forced themselves as masters upon those who had come before.

Priests' homes, walled of stone and shaped like boats, stood near the statued platforms. In these buildings were the "talking boards," tablets and rods of wood inscribed with writing. From these the masters of recitation could call forth the ancient hymns and legends, following the winding current of carved birds and fish, of shellfish and plants that flowed back and forth in a stream across the polished surface of brown-grained wood.

On rocks beside a volcanic crater were engraved the images of the *bird-man*, a giant beaked head upon a human frame. Once every year when sooty terns laid their eggs on a rocky islet off the coast, clan chieftains chose champions to climb down the steep cliff and swim the turbulent, shark-infested sea to reach the birds' nesting place. He who completed the perilous round-trip first, bearing an unbroken egg, won for his master the revered place of *bird-man* and for his clan a place of honor in the year to come.

For centuries the great stone idols were carved—until the end came. Some say rivalries broke out among the clans in jealous competition over the finite resources the island possessed. Others say a revolt broke out among the people against the oppressive "heavy-set ones" as their demand for more and more idols grew beyond reason and endurance. In defiance, stone picks and axes were thrown down in the quarries beside unfinished statues. Hundreds of idols were left on the slopes to eternally await journeys to altars that would never receive them. Hundreds more were toppled from their platforms, their volcanic hats tumbling and rolling in the dust. Civil war, chaos, and even cannibalism followed.

About a century later—on Easter Sunday, 1722—the Dutch explorer Jacob Roggeveen sighted the island. It was he who gave the island the name by which we know it, "Easter" Island. Coming ashore, he found a demoralized and impoverished people. In 1805, twenty-two islanders were carried off into slavery on an American ship. In 1862, a thousand more were carried off by slavers from Peru. Only one hundred of the captives survived the hard physical labor to which they were subjected. Fifteen were to return to Easter Island, bearing with them the scourge of smallpox contracted on the mainland. When missionaries and settlers from Chile arrived on the island in 1877, only 111 natives survived of the thousands that had once dwelled there.

In the twentieth century, scientific investigators arrived. How and why, they asked, had such mighty monuments arisen in so unexpected a way on a small and remote island? The memory of the surviving islanders proved hazy at best: stories of origins and ancestral wars, stories of how statues walked themselves by magic to where they once stood, to where they now lay. When firewood became scarce, the "talking boards" were burnt. By then they had ceased to talk. Today only twenty-six survive and no native can discern their meaning; linguists are baffled too.

Some years ago in his book, *Kon Tiki,* Norwegian adventurer Thor Heyerdahl showed how long sea voyages of two thousand miles or more could be made on a simple balsa raft.

Later he and a colleague, William Mulloy, even demonstrated how massive idols could have been produced and erected by the islanders long ago. Yet the mystery remains. And even if the "how" can be explained, the "why" eludes us still, the "why" in which resides the fierce and unrequited compulsion that drove people for centuries to thrust massive stone faces at the sky—and then stop.

Katherine Routledge, an English visitor in the early 1900s, felt the power of Easter Island. She wrote:

> The inhabitants of today are less real than the men who have gone; the shadows of the departed builders still possess the land. Voluntarily or involuntarily the sojourner must hold communion with those old workers; for the whole air vibrates with a vast purpose and energy which has been and is no more.[57]

22

The Pyramids of the Maya

Temples in the Jungle

IN THE MOIST and hot jungle of southern Mexico and Guatemala, flesh pulses only to rot. In the dark jade-green tangle of steaming lushness, Death clings to the wet earth, waiting, chorused by the screech of monkeys and the cicada's buzz. Decay is all about, mingled with life. Here only stone does not die, and the stars of the night sky, remote and free. Between them is humanity, caught in time and dissolution. All around, in the leafy rain forest, lurk the hideous masks of the nightmare gods.

A thousand years ago and more, a Central American people called the Maya felt the impulse to reach out to the undying stars. Although they lacked metal tools, they quarried stone. And although they lacked beasts of burden and the wheel, they hauled the blocks in place, piling them one upon the other into lofty pyramid-based temples rising in stepped stages high above the trees. From the temple heights their priest-astronomers, unaided by telescopes, tracked the paths of planets and stars and invented a mathematics of time, enshrined in squared hieroglyphic symbols and a calendar of studied intricacy. With stunning accuracy they measured the cosmic year, predicted the eclipses of sun and moon, and even calculated the orbital period of Venus.

In jungle clearings their sacred cities rose in profusion,

Nineteenth-century view of the ruins of Palenque.

rich in plume-bearing priests and painted shrines, proud chieftains and plans for glory. And then, mysteriously, the cities were abandoned. Slowly, inexorably, the jungle claimed its own, shrouding the deserted temples in dark foliage, choking with thick vines the stone-carved icons of nobles and gods.

Centuries later, when the Spaniards came to America, word of the lost cities reached their ears. By then even the names of the cities had been forgotten. But because the cities had no gold, they held little interest for greedy conquerors. To the missionaries the scrolls that had been kept by natives as heirlooms seemed works of the Devil and were summarily burnt; and so in the smoke of a single bonfire vanished the legacy of the Mayan sages.

It was not until the nineteenth century that scientists came to explore the land of the Maya. The most notable traveler to the ruins was an American adventurer named John Lloyd Stephens, whose vivid descriptions, illustrated by his friend, English artist Frederick Catherwood, shed bright sunlight on the splendor of this ancient American civilization. Stephens would write the following account:

> The ground was entirely new; there were no guidebooks or guides; the whole was a virgin soil. We could not see ten yards before us, and never knew what we should stumble upon next. At one time we stopped to cut away branches and vines which concealed the face of a monument, and then to dig around and bring to light a fragment, a sculptured corner of which protruded from the earth. I leaned over with breathless anxiety while the Indians worked, and an eye, an ear, a foot, or a hand was disentombed; and when the machete rang against the chiselled stone, I pushed the Indians away, and cleared out the loose earth with my hands. The beauty of the sculpture, the solemn stillness of the woods, disturbed only by the scrambling of monkeys and the chattering of parrots, the desolation of the city, and the mystery that hung over it, all created an interest higher, if possible, than I had ever felt among the ruins of the Old World.[58]

Many could hardly believe that the spectacular civilization Stephens had seen was native to America; to some it seemed the glorious vestige of a culture that had migrated in the past from the Mediterranean. Likenesses were noted between the pyramids of America and the pyramids of the ancient Near East. Yet, unlike the pyramids of Egypt, the pyramids of Central America bore no evidence of having served as tombs.

In the decades that followed the publication of Stephens's work, other scholars such as J. Eric Thompson came to study the Mayan ruins and sought to unravel the mystery of their script. As the decipherment proceeded, most of the inscriptions were revealed as records of important dates in the history of Mayan culture. But the vital substance of that history remained obscure, as did the reasons for the culture's fall. Had there been a peasant revolt against a tyrannical hierarchy? Had foreign armies invaded? Had widespread disease or famine struck the people? Whatever the reasons, the spiritual force finally ebbed that had held the jungle back as human beings reached out for the stars.

*　　*　　*　　*

Described as the most exquisitely conceived of all Mayan cities, the ruins of Palenque are set upon a high plateau overlooking a plain. Behind the city is the tropical forest of the Chiapas mountains. Here the heaviest rains in all Mexico fall. As light rain drifts over the mountains, a green mist hangs over the limestone ruins.

The site covers some fifteen square miles, though today only the most prominent monuments are visible. Raised on a platform at the center of a broad plaza is a residence building called *El Palacio* (The Palace), a complex of chambers, vaulted galleries, and courtyards. The most striking feature is a four-story tower that may have been used for astronomical observations or to sight visitors approaching from afar. Around the great palace are five temples, set on pyramid-shaped bases and approached by long flights of stairs. At one time, the structures were bright with painted plaster, and from each roof rose a decorative stuccoed "comb" made of limestone. No evidence survives to tell us what gods were worshiped here; two of the temples bear a symbol in the form of a cross—one of which is foliated with leaves—of a tree of life, perhaps, or a great maize plant, symbolic of fertility. One sanctuary is called the Temple of the Count, a name it received from the visit of an aristocratic traveler named Frederick Waldeck, who lived in it for three years while studying Mayan art in the nineteenth century. At one time John Lloyd Stephens even contemplated buying the entire site (he had already paid fifty dollars for the Mayan city of Copan) but was dissuaded by the legal necessity of having to take a native wife.

The tallest temple at Palenque originally rose over one hundred feet above the plaza. Called the Temple of the Inscriptions, it contains one of the longest surviving Mayan texts. Carved on three stone wall-panels at the back of the sanctuary's central chamber is an inscription composed of over six hundred glyphs.

The pyramid temple had a special fascination for twentieth-century archaeologist Alberto Ruz Lhuillier. Ruz was drawn to the Temple of the Inscriptions because it was the most magnificent structure at Palenque. He wondered if, like other Mesoamerican pyramids, it might contain other even older pyramids within its outer structure. (The Mayans had periodically enlarged their pyramids by building larger pyramids over earlier smaller ones.) The core of the Temple of the Inscriptions had never been probed, even though the monument had been visited by all the great explorers of Mayan culture.

As Ruz stood in the temple's vestibule in the spring of 1949 he noticed curious holes in one of the paving blocks in the floor. At each end of the block he spied a series of holes filled with stone plugs or stoppers. Ruz's curiosity was further aroused by the fact that the floor itself was unusual: most Mayan sanctuary floors were stuccoed not paved. Also, the seams in the blocks in the surrounding walls continued *below* the apparent floor level.

Calling in his workers, Ruz ordered the stoppers removed

and the block lifted by what seemed to be holes drilled for this very purpose. When the paving stone was raised, clay and stone rubble were found beneath. Yet as the rubble was painstakingly removed, the stone capstone of a vault was discovered. Beneath that Ruz found the top of a stone-cut step: he had discovered a hidden staircase within the pyramid! But where did it lead?

As the days wore on and densely packed rubble was removed, a steep staircase was uncovered that descended to the west. By the end of the first excavation season in July, a total of twenty-three steps had been cleared. The next season revealed twenty-three more steps and a floor level from which two galleries opened out. As further digging continued, a second staircase was discovered that led back to the east. Above one of the first steps a box was found made of stone, containing a river stone painted red (the symbolic color of blood, life, and the sunrise) and two carved jade earplugs, worn through the pierced and expanded lobes of the ear by Mayan men.

During the following season of excavation, the second stairway was cleared until a paved floor was reached at approximately ground level. At one end was a wall and at its foot another stone box, containing pottery dishes perhaps once filled with offerings, two shells filled with a natural red dye called cinnabar, seven jade beads, a pair of circular jade earplugs carved in the form of flowers, and a half-inch-long tear-shaped pearl. Behind the wall a corridor continued. To the left, near the corridor's end, was a triangular slab—a doorway, but leading where? Before the doorway lay a small grave containing the remains of six skeletons. One skeleton was of a woman; the others, of men. The best preserved of the male skulls bore the deliberate cranial deformation and the filed teeth characteristic of aristocratic Mayan tradition. Slowly, the triangular slab was levered open and Ruz stepped inside. Here is how he described it:

> I . . . found myself in an enormous crypt which seemed to have been cut out of the rock—or rather, out of the ice, thanks to the curtain of stalactites and the chalcite veiling

deposited on the walls by the infiltration of rain-water
during the centuries. This increased the marvelous quality
of the spectacle and gave it a fairy-tale aspect. Great
figures of priests modelled in stucco a little larger than
life-size formed an impressive procession around the
walls. The high vaulting was reinforced by great stone
transoms, of dark color with yellowish veins, giving an
impression of polished wood.

Almost the whole crypt was occupied by a colossal
monument, which we then supposed to be a ceremonial
altar, composed of a stone of more than 8 square metres,
resting on an enormous monolith of 6 cubic metres, supported in its turn by six great blocks of chiselled stone. All
these elements carried beautiful reliefs. I [had] entered the
mysterious chamber with the strange sensation natural for
the first one to tread the entrance steps in a thousand
years. I tried to see it all with the same vision that the
Palenque priests had when they left the crypt; I wanted
to efface the centuries and hear the vibrations of the last
human voices beneath these massive vaults; I strove to
capture the cryptic message that those men of old had
given us so inviolate. Across the impenetrable veil of time
I sought the impossible bond between their lives and
ours.[59]

Ruz now stood some seventy-five feet below the top level
of the pyramid, almost directly beneath its apex. At the
chamber's center was the "altar," tabled by a horizontal slab
of carved limestone 12' 6" long, 7' 2" wide, and 8 inches
thick, described by its discoverer as "one of the most valuable masterpieces of American pre-Hispanic culture."[60] Its
edges were decorated with calendar hieroglyphs; its top surface showed a man reclining on a skull-like mask looking up
toward the trunk of a great plant surmounted by a great
bird. Ruz depicts the scene as follows:

We see a man surrounded by astronomical signs sym-
bolising heaven—the spatial limit of man's earth, and the

home of the gods, in which the unchanging course of the stars marks the implacable rhythm of time. Man rests on the earth, represented by a grotesque head with funereal traits, since the earth is a monster devouring all that lives; and if the reclining man seems to be falling backwards, it is because it is his inherent destiny to fall to the earth, the land of the dead. But above the man rises the well-known cruciform motif, which in some representations is a tree, in others the stylised maize plant, but is always the symbol of life resurgent from the earth, life triumphing over death.[61]

To determine if the block upon which the great slab rested was solid, Ruz ordered it drilled. The drill bored through the stone and then thrust into empty space: the block was hollow. As the drill pulled out, it emerged coated with red ceremonial powder, signifying a burial within.

Ruz ordered the slab cover raised. Slowly, ever so slowly, the five-ton slab was lifted by jacks. Beneath appeared a fish-shaped outline cut in the block and fitted with its own stone cover, drilled and stoppered like the slab in the temple vestibule above.

What Ruz had uncovered was a sarcophagus, the first and only burial ever found within a Mayan pyramid, the sepulcher of a mighty priest-king over whose grave the pyramid had been built. In the hieroglyphic inscription the ruler was named Pacal (Shield), a man who had lived—again according to the deciphered glyphs—in the seventh century A.D. Here in Mexico, over three thousand years after the great pyramid tombs of Egypt had been built, a Mayan potentate had been entombed with similar monumental majesty. The discovery constituted "the most important discovery ever made in Maya archaeology,"[62] and "probably the most dramatic in all American archaeology,"[63] "the most extraordinary tomb so far discovered in this continent of America."[64]

In November 1952, four years after discovering the trapdoor and secret staircase, Ruz ordered the lid raised. Within the sarcophagus were found Pacal's last remains and the remains of the finery with which he had been buried. His skeleton, tinged in the red cinnabar dye that had once coated his shroud, lay on its back, the bones of a forty-year-old man. Jade ornaments lay where they had fallen as flesh and jewelry-stringing had disintegrated. From Pacal's earlobes had once hung flower-shaped earplugs of carved jade with mother-of-pearl backings. Across his neck and chest rested an elaborately beaded jade collar and a pectoral composed of nine concentric rings of jade beads. Jade bracelets had adorned his arms. On each finger was a great jade ring (on one a man crouches in obeisance). Clutched in his right hand was a great cubical jade bead; in his left, a great spherical one: mystical symbols of the universe. In his mouth a jade bead had been placed, perhaps intended to pay for passage to the afterlife.

Most stunning of all was a mosaic mask made of two hundred pieces of jade set in stucco. The eyes, formed of white shell plaques, were inset with irises of black volcanic glass. The mask bears the features that Pacal must have once possessed, features also magnificently expressed in two sculptured portrait heads found buried beneath the mighty sarcophagus.

Near the sarcophagus, a serpent, molded of plaster, climbs along the floor to the chamber's threshold. There, it is transformed into a stone pipe that ascends along the edge of the hidden staircase, step by step, to the temple floor above. Through this conduit, voices of the living could travel from the top of the pyramid to the secret crypt where Pacal's spirit lived. Through this conduit the voice of Pacal's spirit could also rise to the world above.

Beneath the jungle heat in a chamber of limestone ice he had rested for all those centuries, the droplets of water forming and falling in the darkness and silence as the retinue of priests looked on.

> That sunny dome! those caves of ice!
> And all who heard should see them there,
> And all should cry, Beware! Beware!

His flashing eyes, his floating hair!
Weave a circle round him thrice,
And close your eyes with holy dread,
For he on honey-dew hath fed,
And drunk the milk of Paradise.[65]

Secrets of Chichén Itzá

The Well of Sacrifice

ACROSS THE GREAT PLAZA the Mayan procession moved slowly in the heat. Weeks of drought had cracked the fields and baked the earthen pavement dry. Only the sacrifice of a human life could appease the rain god Chac.

At the end of the thousand-foot processional way the congregation stopped. The people of Chichén Itzá had come to the shrine beside the great dark pool. Only then did the drums and the clattering copper bells fall silent. As the blue smoke of incense rose into the motionless summer air, the priest began the prayer.

It was then that the bound victim was brought to the edge of the sacred well to look into its mouth. Sixty-five feet below the round limestone rim, the water waited like a black mirror. Around the dark edges of its surface one could see the disembodied faces of the living circling above, leaning over its gaping one-hundred-eighty-foot mouth.

Then the scream of the victim, flung by the priests into the air and tumbling downward, down into the watery mirror, shattering the black glass of its surface, shattering into a million separate splashes the watery night of noon and the faces that watched . . .

Slowly, ever so slowly, as the victim's struggles finally

Jadeite pendant from the sacred well at Chichén Itzá.

ended, the surface calmed and healed into a black mirror once again, and the procession returned to the plaza from which it had come.

> Into this Well they have had and still have the custom of throwing men alive as a sacrifice to their gods in time of drought, and they believed that they would not die, though they never saw them again. They also threw in many other things like precious stones and things they prized.[66]

So reported Father Diego de Landa, Bishop of Yucatan, in the sixteenth century. Another Spanish report told of women being offered to the god who dwelt at the bottom of the well.

*   *   *   *

In 1885 an American named Edward Herbert Thompson was appointed United States consul in the Yucatan. From his student days at Harvard University, Thompson had been intrigued by the discovery of Mayan ruins and by the theory that Mayan civilization might actually have been founded by survivors of the lost kingdom of Atlantis. During his diplomatic service in Mexico, he purchased for seventy-five dollars the ruins of Chichén Itzá, where he proceeded to take up residence and raise his family.

Knowing the Spanish tales and longing to explore the depths of the sacred well, he returned to Boston to undertake training as a deep-sea diver. Next he succeeded in winning the financial backing of two learned societies for an expedition. In 1904 he returned to the ruined city with a diving suit, two Greek sponge divers, and dredging equipment: a derrick, a hand-operated windlass, and a steel-jawed scoop.

Called a *cenote* (pronounced *say-nó-tay*) by the natives, the sacred well was a sinkhole formed by the collapse of the limestone crust that overlay the underground water of the region. To determine where to dredge, Thompson made wooden dummies the approximate size and weight of local Indians. He then threw the dummies into the pool and marked where they hit. It was in that promising "fertile zone" that Thompson decided to concentrate his dredging operations.

As work commenced, the scoop brought up only rocks, tree trunks, and animal bones mixed with muck and occasional bits of broken pottery. Then one day Thompson spied in the scoop what looked like two yellow ostrich eggs. The "eggs" turned out to be balls of copal incense. When lit, the copal gave off its ancient aroma for Thompson just as it had for priests a thousand years before.

As the dredging continued, the scoop brought up other objects thrown into the well by worshipers: temple vases and incense burners, arrowheads and lance points, beads of jade, gilded copper bells, disks and pendants of beaten gold embossed with images of warriors, and statuettes of Mayan gods. The clappers of the bells had been deliberately removed—and the figurines deliberately broken—to ritually "kill" them so as to release their spirits to travel with the sacrificial victim to Chac's underwater home.

Deciding to explore the depths of the well in person, Thompson donned his diving suit and prepared to make his first descent into the dark waters.

As I stepped on the first rung of the ladder, each of the pumping gang . . . left his place in turn and with a very solemn face shook hands with me and then went back again to wait for the signal. It was not hard to read their thoughts. They were bidding me a last farewell, never expecting to see me again. Then, releasing my hold on the ladder, I sank like a bag of lead, leaving behind me a silvery chain of bubbles. During the first ten feet of descent, the light rays changed from yellow to green and then to a purplish black. After that I was in utter darkness. . . . On the bottom . . . as I stood on the flat end of a big stone column, ... I realized that I was the only living being who had ever reached this place alive and expected to leave it again still living.[67]

Groping through water and mud seventy feet deep, Thompson found that his underwater flashlight could not penetrate the darkness, or what lurked within it.

The present natives of the region believe that big snakes and strange monsters live in the dark depths of the Sacred Well. Whether this belief is due to some faint remembrance of the old serpent worship, or is based upon something seen by some of the natives, can only be guessed at. I have seen big snakes and lizards swimming in these waters, but they were only snakes and lizards that in chasing their prey through the trees above had fallen into the pool and were trying to get out. We saw no traces of any reptiles or monsters of unusual size anywhere in the pool.

No strange reptile ever got me in its clutches, but I had one experience that is worth repeating. Both of us, the Greek diver and I, were busily digging with our fingers in a narrow crevice of the floor and it was yielding such rich returns that we neglected some of our usual precautions. Suddenly I felt something over me, an enormous something that with a stealthy, gliding movement was pressing down on me. Something smooth and slimy was pushing me irresistibly into the mud. For a moment my blood ran cold. Then I felt the Greek beside me pushing at an object and I aided him until we had worked ourselves free. It was the decaying trunk of a tree that had drifted off the bank of mud and in sinking had encountered my stooping body.[68]

Among the objects Thompson would recover during three years of diving and dredging were the poignant human remains of sacrificial victims: skeletons of thirteen men, eight women, and twenty-one children. Children had been the prime offering to win the rain god's favor. The children had died between the ages of eighteen months and twelve years; about half had been sacrificed when they were less than six years old. Indeed, because children's skulls survive less readily than adults', young children probably constituted an even larger proportion of victims than the evidence shows. Of the eight women, seven had been over the age of twenty-one. During a dive Thompson came upon a group of three victims, fragments of their garments still clinging to their skeletons; around the neck of one lay the jade pendants of the necklace she had once worn. That a priest may have slipped or been pushed into the well by a victim is suggested by the curious discovery of an old man's skull among the bones.

Of the artifacts found by Thompson, most were sent in discreet diplomatic pouches to Harvard's Peabody Museum, much to the later consternation of Mexican authorities who felt they had been robbed of an important part of their historical heritage. Though the museum would relinquish a portion of this collection decades later, the bulk of Thompson's finds still resides in Cambridge, Massachusetts.

In 1960, to correct this deficit, Mexican enthusiasts made new efforts to probe Chichén Itzá's sacred well. The expedition, undertaken by the Exploration and Water Sports Club of Mexico with the support of the National Geographic Society, employed a device called an "air lift." It operates like an underwater vacuum cleaner, sucking up water, silt, and small objects through an intake pipe and spewing them onto a screen mounted on a barge where the finds can be inspected. Below, at water's bottom, scuba divers direct the intake pipe to the areas being excavated. The Mexican expedition recovered over four thousand artifacts including objects of jade, amber, and crystal, a sacrificial bone knife with handle covered in gold foil, and ritual figurines made out of latex rubber. The expedition also recovered stones that had fallen into the water from the sanctuary above, where parts of the limestone edge had collapsed, and succeeded in mapping the contours of the well's bottom. Seven years later, pumping operations lowered the water level in the cenote and more than six thousand additional artifacts were recovered. Among them were the first pieces of Mayan furniture ever discovered, two ornately carved wooden stools, and the gold-foil soles of a child-sized pair of sandals. In the mud the divers also found the bones of four to five hundred more sacrificial victims.

*   *   *   *

Across the great plaza the tourist procession moved slowly in the heat. Only the refreshing drinks of the hotel bars had brought relief.

At the end of the thousand-foot processional way the group stopped. The tourists had come to the shrine beside the great dark well. Only then did the men with their clicking cameras and the women chattering over souvenirs fall silent as the hired guide began his talk.

A piece of spent chewing gum, flung by someone into the air and tumbling downward, plopped into the surface of the black pool, stirring in it an ancient hunger. Slowly, ever so slowly, as the tourists returned to their dusty bus, the ripples ceased. The drought would continue for many more days.

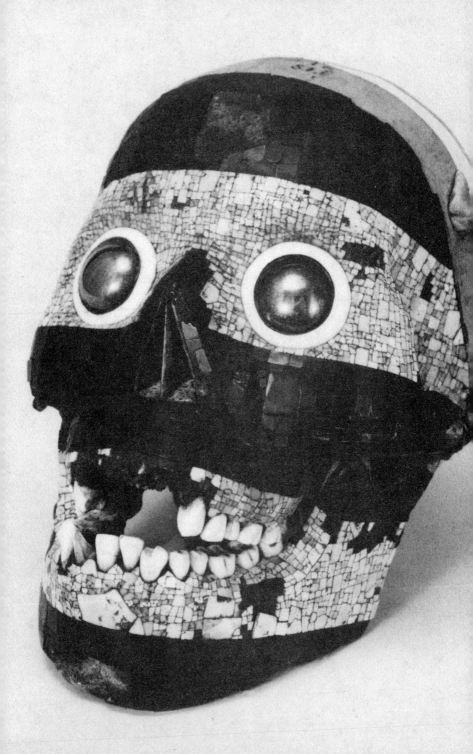

24

The Empire of the Aztecs

Blood on the Sun

THE SPANISH SOLDIER, bent with age, held pen in arthritic hand as he sat before a simple desk. The year was 1576: the place, Mexico. "I am an old man now," he wrote, "over eighty-four years of age, and I have lost my sight and hearing, and, as luck would have it, I have gained nothing of value to leave to my children and descendants but this my true story, and they will presently find out what a wonderful story it is."[69]

The soldier's name was Bernal Díaz del Castillo. As a young man he had fought in over a hundred battles as a simple foot soldier beside the great Cortés. Now before his death he would tell his story, the story of how a small band of Spanish adventurers had brought crashing down the mighty empire of the Aztecs.

Díaz was born in 1492, the very year Christopher Columbus discovered a New World for Spain. It was a time of intense patriotism, for in that same year Moslem invaders were driven from Granada.

In the bright morning of the sixteenth century life was exhilarating in the Spanish Peninsula, for it seemed to hold a richer promise for mankind than ever before in human history. The rapid emergence of Spain as one of

Aztec mask made from a human skull.

the first modern nations had coincided with the realization that the habitable world was a vaster space than heretofore conceived. This sudden expansion of horizons to unbelievable dimensions, intellectual as well as physical, was now coupled with a sense of destiny as the appointed agent of God for the tremendous task of Christianizing the globe. Was not the final crushing victory over the Moors after nearly eight centuries of warfare a sign of divine approval? And were not the discoveries of Columbus at the same time clear indications of the special approbation of Providence? The Spaniard could not but feel himself very precious in the eyes of the Lord, as he easily conceived his people as the chosen race of the Almighty. This conviction released a prodigious national energy and powerfully stimulated the passionate imagination of youth.

To be young in the Hispanic Peninsula during this period of human experience was to have faith in the impossible. An enormously enlarged world teemed with possibilities of adventure, riches, and romance in which the wildest dreams and the fondest hopes of fame and fortune might be fulfilled.[70]

Led on by the lust for God and gold, the Spaniards came to the New World. They found more than enough natives to convert to God's worship but—alas—little treasure. Frustrated by the poverty of Columbus's finds, many a Spaniard looked to farther horizons.

One such man was the young Hernando Cortés. Fed by rumors of fabulous wealth in the unexplored land of Mexico, Cortés in 1519 set sail from Cuba as commander of a new expedition to the west. He brought with him seven hundred men on eleven ships.

Cortés's flotilla awed the natives, who called the ships "mountains that move." Never having seen a horse before, they regarded the Spanish mounts as monsters with human torsos growing from four legs. The natives were also frightened by Cortés's deadly firepower that included muskets and cannon, believing the explosions were the voices of evil spirits (as indeed they were).

The Spanish cause was aided by the cruel imperialism of the Aztecs. Because of this imperialism, thousands of subject tribesmen joined Cortés in making war against their hated overlords.

The Spaniards were also aided by native religion. According to legend, a god had once come in human form, white-skinned, bearded, and dressed in black. Named Quetzal-cóatl, the god had bestowed great wisdom upon the people. Then he sailed away to his home in the east, vowing one day to return and rule. Tradition held that his second coming by sea would occur in a "one-reed year," a calendric event that came once every fifty-two years. It was Cortés's luck that 1519 was such a year. In the eyes of the natives, bearded Cortés—white-skinned and dressed in black—was the longed-for Messiah returning at the prophesied time. On news of his landing, the Aztec emperor sent ambassadors to Cortés with gifts of gold—precisely what this Messiah had wanted, and craved more of.

At the place he had landed on Good Friday, 1519, Cortés planted a colony, Villa Rica de Vera Cruz (The Rich City of the True Cross). Then, to prevent a change of heart among his men, Cortés boldly ordered his entire fleet scuttled and prepared to march on the Aztec capital.

> Thus, in August, 1519, this extraordinary young man set off without maps across an unknown country, against an empire of apparently limitless power, wealth, and savagery, never knowing what lay beyond the next hill except that he would probably be encountering armies many times stronger than his own and almost certainly hostile.[71]

Finally, descending from a twelve-thousand-foot mountain pass, Cortés and his men looked down to see spread out before them on the sparkling surface of a lake the shimmering image of a vast city. "We were amazed," Bernal Díaz recalled, "and said that it was like the enchantments they tell of in the legend of Amadis, on account of the great towers and palaces and cues [temples] and buildings rising from the water, and all built of masonry. And some of our soldiers even asked whether the things that we saw were not a dream."[72]

They entered the city unopposed. Borne in a rich litter, the Aztec emperor Montezuma came to greet these visitors from another world, welcoming them to his city.

As Cortés and his men crossed the great plaza, they beheld a fearful symbol of Aztec power: a platform fitted with vertical poles holding the stacked-up skulls of sacrificial victims. Rising above the plaza was a great pyramidal temple surmounted by twin shrines to the gods of war and life-giving rain. Within was evidence of the Aztecs' savagery. Díaz reports: "They [the priests] saw open the chest [of a human victim] with stone knives and hasten to tear out the palpitating heart and blood, and offer it to their Idols. . . . They cut off the thighs . . . and eat [them] at feasts. . . . All the walls of the oratory were so splashed and encrusted with blood that they were black, the floor was the same and the whole place stunk vilely."[73]

The human victims for these rites were prisoners of war or were taken by force from the tribute-paying tribes over whom the Aztecs ruled. Twenty thousand victims are said to have been slaughtered in that year alone.

Such sacrifices were central to Aztec religion. According to Aztec belief, Tonatiuh, the god of the sun, was nourished by human blood. It was the duty of humankind to provide this blood lest the cruel sun god fulfill his threat to shine no more. On a massive twenty-five-ton sacrificial disc of stone the grinning face of Tonatiuh looked out, surrounded by the hieroglyphic symbols of cosmic time.

Montezuma did not fear the godlike strangers. Certainly he did not fear for his own life, since the emperor's person was inviolate. He welcomed the Spaniards graciously, and in turn Cortés extended his own courtesy, offering the emperor the privilege of being placed under house arrest or being killed—a most unexpected response, but one peculiarly effective in controlling the entire population.

Montezuma would eventually die, but at the hands of his own people who believed him a traitor. Then, in the dead of night, Cortés and his men would attempt escape across the lagoons. Half would die, most killed by attacking natives, but many drowned from the weight of Aztec gold stuffed into their pockets.

Yet Cortés himself would not give up. At a safe distance, he ordered the construction of a portable fleet and, reinforced by ten thousand Indian allies, marched back to Tenochtitlán. After a three-month naval siege, the Aztecs, weakened by an outbreak of smallpox, surrendered.

Cortés ordered the city systematically dismembered, stone by stone. "I say again that I stood looking at it," Díaz wrote, "and thought that never in the world would there be discovered other lands such as these. . . . Of all these wonders that I then beheld today all is overthrown and lost, nothing left standing."[74]

The golden treasures of the Aztecs were shipped back to Spain. In Renaissance Europe, German artist Albrecht Dürer marveled at the objects he inspected.

> I have also seen the things that were brought to the King from the new Golden Land: a sun entirely of gold, a whole fathom broad; and a silver moon, just as big; and two rooms full of armor; and all kinds of arms, harnesses, and wonderful missiles; very strange clothing, bed-gear, and all kinds of the most wonderful things for man's use, that are as beautiful to behold as they are wonderful. These things are all so costly that they have been valued at a hundred thousand guilders. And I have never in all the days of my life seen anything that has so much rejoiced my heart as these things. For I have seen among them wonderfully artistic things, and have marvelled at the subtle genius of men in foreign lands. I have no words to express my feelings at what I saw.[75]

The Spanish court did not share Dürer's respect for the artistry of the Aztecs. In the atmosphere of the Inquisition the pagan curiosities were idols to be destroyed. Furthermore, the Spanish king had more interest in bullion than in *objets d'art.* As a consequence, almost the entire legacy of Aztec art was thrown into the melting pot.

Those objects that did survive were made of less precious stuff: feathers, turquoise, and shell; a mosaic mask of the sun god; a priest's green-feathered headdress; a sacrificial knife of stone. The most macabre relic is a gift from Montezuma to Cortés: a leather-lined mask made from half a human skull. The teeth, in a movable jaw hinged in leather, are still in place; the face, banded in turquoise and black. From eye-sockets rimmed in white shell gleam golden spheres of iron pyrite, "fool's gold."

Cortés was to profit little from the treasure he stole. Given only empty honors by a jealous court, he would die in poverty. A story tells how once in later years he fought his way through a crowd to reach and mount the royal carriage. "Who are you?" the surprised king asked. "I am a man," said Cortés, "who has given you more provinces than your ancestors left you cities." We are told that the king merely said, "Drive on."

*   *   *   *

Over the ruins of ancient Tenochtitlán now rise the buildings of modern Mexico City: on the foundations of a pagan shrine stands a great cathedral; on the fallen halls of Montezuma, a presidential palace. Recent excavations in the heart of Mexico City have revealed beneath an entire city block the awesome outlines of the temple where tens of thousands were once sacrificed to sustain the god of the sun. Powerful sculptures of the gods have been found beside the buried skulls of sacrificial victims, stone knives still stuck in the bone, yellow incense still staining the eye sockets.

Long ago an Aztec wrote the following poem:

> With tears and flowers of grief
> I, the poet,
> compose my song.
> I think

of those
who broken and shattered lie
in the realm of the dead.
They came
to be lords and rulers
on earth.
Like tattered feathers,
like shattered precious stone,
they lie in the dust.[76]

25

The Kingdom of the Incas

Child of the Andes

HELD HIGH OVER the priest's head—its strands held taut from hand to hand—the rope of Inca gold glowed in the rays of the dying sun. The priest stood on the altar at the edge of the abyss, facing the western sky. For weeks, night had come sooner and sooner; for weeks, the sun's path had sunk lower in the sky. Chanting, he pleaded with the sun not to leave the world in darkness, not to forsake mankind. Taking the golden rope, he tied it round the stone post, magically binding the sun to the earth.

*   *   *   *

High in the Peruvian Andes lie the ruins of Machu Picchu. Hung two thousand feet above the green lushness of the Urubamba gorge, the city floats in mist halfway between heaven and earth. Hewn of granite, its buildings spill out across a grassy saddle of land between mountain peaks. A hundred staircases cascade to the city's edges where gentle terraces, walled in stone, slumber on airy slopes.

Ever since its discovery in 1911 by American explorer Hiram Bingham, the meaning of Machu Picchu has been a mystery. Was it military fortress or sacred citadel? When was it built and why was it abandoned? Indeed, even the city's true name is unknown.

Panoramic view of Machu Picchu.

What *is* known is that it was built by the Incas, the most powerful nation of ancient South America. By the sixteenth century the Incas had—in only decades—constructed a continental empire that stretched for twenty-five hundred miles, from Ecuador in the north to Chile in the south. Their capital at Cuzco still endures as the oldest continuously inhabited city in the New World.

Although the Incas lacked wheeled vehicles and the horse, their communications system was formidable, linked by a network of paved roads eleven-thousand miles in length. Rest houses were provided for travelers at regular intervals, while government relay runners, stationed every two miles, speedily carried messages to and from administrative centers, sometimes by crossing daring suspension bridges of rope.

It is extraordinary that the civilized Incas possessed no system of writing. Instead, messages were carried by memory. Complex information was recorded and stored in ingenious data banks called *quipus,* elaborate sets of colored and intricately knotted strings that could be decoded by skilled "rememberers."

The government was a rigidly structured bureaucracy directed by the divine emperor, a descendant of the sun god. The economy was communally organized around the clan, with all able-bodied workers contributing to projects in the service of the state, which in turn provided the individual with security.

Terracing enhanced the productivity of the land, permitting steeply sloped mountain terrain to be farmed in level steps irrigated by artificial waterfalls fed by aqueducts. Corn and potatoes were the staples of the Inca diet, both unknown in Europe at the time. From corn the Incas made a kind of beer called *chicha,* often used in ceremonies. Potatoes, available in several varieties, were preserved by a process of freeze-drying in which water was eliminated from crushed pulp by high-altitude coldness.

The everyday life of the Incas, their history and their customs, are recorded in narratives written in the century after the Spanish conquest. Of these narratives the two most important were composed by men of mixed parentage, their mothers Peruvian, their fathers Spanish: *The Royal Commentaries of the Inca* by Garcilaso de la Vega and *New Chronicles and Good Government* by Felipe Guaman Poma de Ayala. The latter is richly illustrated with drawings of Inca life.

But the humanity of this ancient people is conveyed even more graphically by a discovery made in 1954 on an eighteen-thousand-foot Chilean mountaintop. There in a simple crypt on the summit, relic hunters found the frozen body of an Inca boy. His knees were tucked into his chest; his arms, wrapped round his legs for warmth. His face rested on his knees just as it had when he fell asleep five hundred years before. On his face, ceremonial paint and powder were still visible and came off at a touch. The boy was only eight or nine years old.

A black, llama-wool tunic, fringed in red, covered his frail body. Condor feathers still clung to his woolen headdress. A bracelet circled one wrist and slippers covered his feet. Heavy calluses suggested he had walked hundreds of miles from Peru to reach the mountain. Chicha beer would have been given to him to make him sleepy until cold numbed his senses. There, on the summit, the priests would have then left him as a sacrifice to the god of the sun.

At the boy's feet lay a small golden llama and the golden figurine of a god dressed in wool. On the god's head was a feather headdress, still radiant in yellow and red. Ritual pouches contained the boy's nail parings and baby teeth. In another pouch were coca leaves, the source of cocaine. Chewed by the natives of ancient South America for their stimulant effect, the leaves would have helped the boy stave off hunger and cold during the long march.

Taken down on mule-back to Santiago, the boy of Cerro el Plomo was put in a refrigerated showcase in Chile's National Museum of Natural History. There he was to rest for almost thirty years until the museum staff noticed cracks forming on his hands and feet. Concerned about deterioration, they appealed to UNESCO for help and welcomed an international team of scientists to Chile.

The head of the UNESCO team, Canadian histologist Patrick Horne, soon determined the cause of the problem: the cracking was due to temperature change. Despite the fact that Santiago had frequent electrical blackouts, the showcase was not equipped with an emergency generator to maintain constant cold. Instead, the repeated rise and fall in temperature had caused the boy's flesh to expand and contract over and over again until it cracked. In addition, the uncontrolled humidity in the showcase had allowed the growth of bacteria and fungi. The solution: install a backup generator and a dehumidifier.

Two by-products emerged from the study of the Inca boy's skin. Curious growths on the boy's thigh—angiokeratomas—led the researchers to speculate that this peculiar condition may have marked the boy as special and may have caused him to be chosen for sacrifice. Second, a growth that looked like a wart was examined by electron microscope and found to be just that, a wart—a seemingly trivial finding but one that demonstrated for the first time that viruses existed in America before the coming of European colonists.

*   *   *   *

Despite the prayers of priests and the sacrifice of children, the sun did eventually set on the Inca empire. In a volley of gunfire that slaughtered an unarmed retinue, Francisco Pizarro in 1532 captured the unsuspecting emperor Atahualpa and with him the empire. Held hostage, the emperor offered a ransom: he would fill the spacious room in which he was imprisoned as high as the hand could reach with gold.

From all quarters of the empire the treasure was brought. Even Cuzco's dazzling Temple of the Sun was stripped of its golden veneer. In six months, eleven tons of gold filled the room. It was now Pizarro's move, and move he did, ordering the emperor garroted from a stake.

Though guerrilla war would ensue for forty years, the Spanish had triumphed. Not even the massive fortress of Sacsahuaman, overlooking Cuzco, could stop them. Its bulging, hundred-ton blocks of stone, angled together with such precision that even the thinnest knife blade cannot pass between them, proved an empty boast.

Fifty miles to the north on the heights of Machu Picchu, a site never discovered by the Spaniards, the priests continued to pray until hope itself died. In time, the last of the Chosen Women, consecrated to the sun god, perished, and were buried in their cliffside graves. The temples lay abandoned—the sacred *intihuatana* stone, "hitching-post of the sun," a gray silhouette against the sky.

Today Peru is sustained by tourism, that ultimate humiliation of a conquered civilization. More tourist dollars flow into Peru each year than all of Atahualpa's ransom. A hundred thousand visitors a year come to Machu Picchu, a number that will soon double. Hiking with backpack or trekking by train, they come bearing litter and seeking souvenirs. As Oscar Wilde remarked: "All men kill the thing they love."

At dusk, when the last bus has zigzagged down the course of the Hiram Bingham Highway, a chill wind sweeps across the ruins. Far to the south in the darkness of a Santiago museum, the compressor hums as an ancient child sleeps, guarded by a golden llama.

Ætatis suæ 21. Aº. 1616.

Matoaks als Rebecka daughter to the mighty Prince
Powhatan Emperour of Attanoughkomouck als Virginia
converted and baptized in the Christian faith, and
Wife to the Worꝰ Mr Tho: Rolff.

26

The World of Jamestown

Portrait of Pocahontas

SHE HELD HER RIGHT HAND just as he had turned it, the handle of the white-feather fan poised between her copper-colored fingers. For more than an hour her head had stayed motionless and level, her large, dark eyes observing him with amused interest as he sketched her portrait.

It was her smile he still struggled to capture. The lace collar she wore, intricate in its starched patterning, had been ready-made for the copyist's hand; its pure geometry was its own betrayal. Even the curving designs that flowed through her red brocade seemed to yield in surrender to his skill. But the smile on those lips still eluded him.

The artist had wondered what he would think of her, what she would think of him, as he had unfolded his easel. Who was she, this young woman so pliant in posing, so proud? Female savage or princess? Wife to an English gentleman or daughter to a savage chief? Could one be both?

They called her Pocahontas. Or so her father, wise Powhatan, had named her when she was still a girl as he watched her spirited ways—Pocahontas, "full of play." Powhatan had fathered twenty sons and eleven daughters, but she was his favorite and she could do no wrong. She would give her friendship, then her brave love, to the alien whitemen who

Portrait of Pocahontas by an unknown artist.

came from across the sea to take land from her people. She would even marry one of the strangers, widower John Rolfe —so guilty he had fallen in love with a savage whose image tormented his lonely nights, so eager to give her baptism to save her soul—and his. She would even go with him to England to live. Had she looked at him also with that same smile when the two had first met in Virginia?

*   *   *   *

The ships that had carried the first English colonists across the great sea were small: the *Discovery* held but twenty-one including the crew; the *Godspeed,* fifty-two; the *Susan Constant,* the largest of the convoy, only seventy-one. It was the year 1607, thirteen years before the Pilgrims, in search of free worship, would touch Plymouth Rock. But these earlier travelers had not come in search of religious freedom. Instead, they had come for profit, intending to stay only so long as it took to become rich.

The English hungered for the same New World gold the Spaniards had already stolen from the tribes of Mexico and Peru. But the English had come late to the feast, and little remained on the table except the lands north of Spanish Florida, lands the English had called "Virginia," in honor of their virgin queen. Inspired by Elizabeth's favorite, Sir Walter Raleigh, English investors had financed a settlement in 1587 on an island called Roanoke, but when a second ship arrived all human trace of the colony had vanished.

Twenty years later, under a new monarch, James I, the Virginia Company of London decided to try once again. The lure of wealth was great enough to overcome the memory of the "lost colony."

After a four-month voyage, the ships reached the "faire, fertill, and well watred countrie" of Virginia and, sailing up what came to be called the James River, found an island that seemed a "verie fit place for erecting a great cittie," a site they would call James' Towne.

All the colonists were ready to get rich quick, but few were prepared for the real New World they found themselves in. Not one was a farmer. The most prominent were city-bred gentlemen, lazy and contemptuous of physical labor. After building a simple fort and making tentative contact with the natives, they busied themselves looking for gold and the long-sought "northwest passage" to the Orient. Precious days were spent in these endeavors, days that could have been used in plowing and sowing for the long stay in what was, despite its elusive beauty, a wilderness in which men could die.

Months after the first glittering ore had been shipped to the motherland with high hopes, a boat returned with news that the rocks were only worthless "fool's gold." A series of grand designs followed, each collapsing in turn. One was a plan to grow and export tropical fruit; another was to grow mulberry bushes to feed silkworms. As each scheme failed, frustration led to bickering and quarrels over leadership.

The site itself, which had seemed like paradise in the springtime of its discovery, soon turned hostile. Wells yielded water that was brackish and foul to drink; in summer the surrounding marshlands bred disease-carrying mosquitoes and other biting insects. By winter, when food supplies had run low, death took such a toll that of the 105 original colonists only 67 remained alive.

It was the firm hand of Captain John Smith that saved the Jamestown colony. Enforcing stern discipline on the surviving colonists, he insisted that building and planting take priority over the search for gold. But an accidental explosion of gunpowder in 1609 forced Smith to return to England for medical attention.

The winter that followed was devastating. Racked by severe cold, disease, and starvation, nine out of every ten colonists died during a period the survivors' annals later recalled as the "starveing Tyme."

Fresh hope was given to the people of Jamestown by the timely arrival of a vessel containing ample supplies and eager new colonists. Yet the true salvation of the Virginia colony came from the discovery of tobacco—a new source of wealth.

The smoking of tobacco was an American Indian custom introduced to European society by Christopher Columbus. Cultivated in America for export to Europe, tobacco soon became a major source of Spanish wealth. To guard their monopoly the Spaniards forbade the exportation of young tobacco plants or seeds from their plantations in the West Indies.

Somehow, however, a Jamestown colonist named John Rolfe obtained some for planting. Tobacco had long been grown by the tribes of Virginia, but was of poor quality compared to the West Indian variety. Rolfe wondered if he might be able to grow the West Indian strain on Virginian soil. His idea worked, and soon Jamestown achieved its first real commercial success. In 1616, just four years after its first experimental crop, the Jamestown colony was able to export twenty-five hundred pounds of tobacco to England. So great did the demand become for the sweet-scented Virginia leaf that forty thousand pounds were soon being shipped annually.

The smoking of tobacco had been popularized in English society by none other than Sir Walter Raleigh. Smoking tobacco had also been promoted by the French ambassador to Portugal, who claimed that tobacco was one of God's greatest gifts to mankind because of what he believed to be its remarkable curative powers. The name of that diplomat, Jean Nicot, would later be immortalized in the word "nicotine."

Not everyone favored smoking, however. None other than King James himself opposed smoking on the grounds of health and morality. In a tract entitled "A Counterblaste to Tobacco," he urged his people:

> Have you not reason then to bee ashamed, and to forbeare this filthie noveltie, so basely grounded, so foolishly received and so grossely mistaken in the right use thereof? . . . A custome lothsome to the eye, hatefull to the Nose, harmefull to the braine, dangerous to the Lungs, and in the blacke stinking fume thereof, neerest resembling the horrible Stigian smoke of the pit that is bottomeless.

But the smoking of tobacco had become too profitable a habit, to the Virginia Company of London and even to the English government itself, which thrived on the taxing of tobacco shipments. In the Virginia colony itself, the taxing of tobacco generated revenues that were in part used to finance the founding of one of the oldest of America's universities, the College of William and Mary in the nearby community of Williamsburg, a college whose distinguished alumni would include Thomas Jefferson, James Monroe, and John Marshall.

Jamestown had become the first permanent English settlement in America. It served as the Virginia colony's first capital, a position it held for almost a century until it was eclipsed by Williamsburg. It was in Jamestown that the first representative assembly in American history met when landowners desirous of home rule formed a House of Burgesses in 1619. (That body still meets in the state of Virginia's present capital, Richmond, as the oldest American legislature in continuous existence.) To Jamestown can also be traced the beginnings of the plantation system in the American South and the first importation of blacks for labor, brought by a Dutch ship from the West Indies.

In its early history the colonists' cause had been aided by the friendship of Pocahontas, daughter of the great chief Powhatan. A story later told by Captain John Smith said she had saved his life once when he was captured by using her own body to protect him from execution. Later held hostage herself by the colonial governor, she came to live in Jamestown and to know its English inhabitants. She was fascinated by the newness of all she saw and eventually chose to tie her destiny to that of the colonists by accepting an offer of marriage from John Rolfe, the man who had won for the colony a new future.

The relations between the Indians and the English had always been uneasy. The Indians had sensed the white man's greed and feared his weapons, but accounted him weak in numbers. As shipload after shipload of new colonists arrived, the Indians' sense of menace grew, held in check only by Powhatan's faith. The prospect of his death presaged bloody confrontation.

Contained in the pages of Captain Smith's *Generall Historie of Virginia* is a list of Indian words learned by the white men. Some, such as *mockasins* and *tomahacks* have long been woven into our heritage. Somewhere else, somewhere hidden among the English meanings of Algonquin words and phrases, halfway between *knives* and *guns,* between *best of friends* and *worst of enemies,* lies the story of Jamestown and the native Americans who first beheld the coming of a new nation. It is a story written in the glossary of village campfires long cold and the embers of cottage timbers set ablaze.

* * * *

The story of archaeology in America began with the most famous graduate of the College of William and Mary, Thomas Jefferson. In 1784 Jefferson's curiosity about Indian mounds in Virginia led him to dig and discover the presence of burials containing skeletons. His surviving notes reveal a deliberate search for knowledge and a careful interpretation of evidence that mark Jefferson as one of the first practitioners of scientific archaeology.

Since Jefferson's day additional burials have been discovered by archaeologists of our own era. Together with colonial descriptions of Indian life and research into tribal memories and traditions, a three-dimensional picture has emerged of the people of Pocahontas. The surviving touchstones of their everyday life are the mortars and pestles used to grind corn into flour and the flint blades of hunting arrows and spears. Found also are stone-carved pipes for the smoking of tobacco. Objects of European manufacture have been discovered at Indian sites too, objects given by the English in trade. Some appealed to the eye, like colorful glass beads; some to the ear, like tiny bells and curious Jew's-harps played on the mouth; some to the hand, like metal knives and that remarkable set of two knives together called a scissor.

In Jamestown itself excavations began about fifty years ago. From the picture of colonial life that has emerged we can recognize the colonists' fear of the known and the unknown. Rusting weapons, lost in skirmishes and raids or buried in the recurrent fires that struck the settlers, convey the range of seventeenth-century European armament: crossbow, cutlass, rapier, and sword; grapeshot for cannon; musket and pistol; bullet molds and bandolier for holding premeasured loads of gunpowder. Recovered four miles downriver from Jamestown is a helmet weighing eight pounds. The most ingenious bit of battle equipment found is one called a *caltrop,* a metal object not unlike a child's jack, cast with four sharp points so that when dropped one point would always face up to cripple a pursuer.

For security the colonists had built a wooden fort soon after they landed. Though remains of the original fort were eventually washed away by the James River, the settlers' own accounts tell us that it was triangular in shape with a watchtower at each corner equipped with cannon. Within the walls were houses, storage facilities, and a chapel. When the settlement developed, a church was built outside the original fort. Of that church only a stone tower remains, the only seventeenth-century structure that still stands amid the ruins of the town. The faith of the people is borne out also by the discovery of a silver communion set with cup and plate and a brass bookbinding clamp, very possibly from a family Bible. It was, incidentally, the same King James for whom Jamestown was named that sponsored the famous 1611 English translation of the Bible that also bears his name.

As the colonists' sense of security increased, homes were built outside the original stockade. Many of their brick foundations have been found. Walls were plastered with lime from ground oyster shells found nearby, and windows were small, composed of diamond-shaped panes of glass held together with wrought iron. Roofing tiles were slate or tile. On one clay tile, set out to dry before being baked, two seventeenth-century dogs have left their paw prints.

In such a home the fireplace would have been the center of life, especially in the cold of winter. Andirons have been found, one type with cherubs' heads, as well as a special iron extension-arm with chain meant to support a pot of hot soup or stew. Many a Jamestown fireplace was framed in delft tiles hand-painted in white and blue. Scenes show children playing, engaged in such pastimes as rolling hoops, skipping rope, spinning tops, and riding their hobbyhorses, children as lively and active as they were centuries ago.

A great variety of cooking and eating utensils have been discovered, some of local manufacture and a number imported. Some of the imported ware is still bright with color: Italian plates painted in yellow, green, and red, and yellow-painted English ware enlivened with red-brown flowers. Thousands of fragments of pottery and porcelain have been found, many from Germany, Holland, Spain, and Portugal. Glass bottles have been found for holding wine or—the then popular European temptation—gin. Many two-tine forks have been unearthed with bone or ivory handles. One of the most precious finds is a pewter spoon handle inscribed with the name of the Virginia artisan who made it, Joseph Copeland, along with the date of manufacture (1675) and the site (Chuckatuck, a settlement about thirty miles southeast of Jamestown). It is the oldest-known surviving example of American pewter.

Among miscellaneous objects discovered are candlesticks and candle snuffers; hinges and drawer handles for wooden furniture long-since decayed, buckles for shoes, and thimbles. One thimble, made of brass, was found still stuffed with the paper that had been used to keep it on the finger of its owner.

Among the most numerous objects found are seventeenth-century clay pipes and pipe fragments. Over fifty thousand bowls, stems, and pieces have been tallied, attesting to the widespread and continuous use of tobacco in the colony. Metal pipe-tongs have also been uncovered, once used to lift glowing embers from fireplaces to light gentlemen's pipes.

The care of the colonists' health and the presence of physicians is evidenced by a surviving lancet, a medicine bottle and vial, an ointment jar, a brass mortar for making medicinal powders, and a set of apothecary scales, including brass pan and weights and an iron balance arm.

Specialized tools, found by archaeologists, reveal the variety of artisans that once plied their trades in Jamestown's heyday: carpenters, barrel makers, boat builders, blacksmiths, shoemakers, armorers, and pipe makers. Jamestown was also the site of America's first industries: iron making and glass-making. Home industries are also revealed, such as spinning and weaving, dairying and cheese making, baking and brewing, farming and fishing. Butcher knives and sheepshears, horseshoes and bridle bits, tell of early Virginia's horses and livestock.

Altogether more than half a million artifacts have been recovered from the soil of Jamestown, evidence of the European culture that had come to the shores of the New World, the culture Pocahontas would come to know and eventually accept as her own.

*　　*　　*　　*

As spring began, Pocahontas was buried. It was the twenty-first of March, 1617, and she was only twenty-two. She had come to England to live there with her husband.

Two years before, she had given birth to a son, a child of two worlds, New and Old, a child called Thomas. The ship that was leaving the docks of London for America would have let his grandfather Powhatan see him for the first time. John Rolfe would return proudly as the Virginia Colony's new Secretary—Pocahontas beside him, home again.

But the journey would end before it had begun. The ship was ordered to stop before it had left the Thames: Pocahontas was too weak to go on. She had been ill during the winter. Some say that the climate of London was unfriendly, that she was killed by its dampness and chill. But it is always hard to move from one world to another.

In a churchyard at Gravesend her body was buried. Recording the burial, the parish register lists a "Rebecca" (the name Pocahontas was given at her baptism), "a Virginia Lady borne."

Before her death a portrait of her had been sketched in London, and from this portrait another was later made in oils for the Rolfe family to own. Some humble objects, said once to have belonged to Pocahontas, were numbered among their heirlooms: a small earthenware vase, a needle case, a basket. A pair of earrings also survived, delicate white shells set in silver.

In Virginia, by the James River, springtime still comes fresh and new. Birds warble as waters lap close by the ruins of shop and home. Far off across the sea in the garden of the Rolfe estate a mulberry tree still grows that Pocahontas once planted with her own hands. Her body rests in an unmarked grave beside the Thames, an ocean apart from old passions and dreams.

Conclusion

In Search of Dreams

OUR LONG JOURNEY now draws to an end. We have traveled across both space and time, across thousands of miles and thousands of years. We have journeyed from the tombs of Egypt to the battlements of Troy, from the shores of the Dead Sea to the streets of Pompeii, from the Great Wall of China to the windswept cliffs of Easter Island, from the caves of prehistoric Europe to the New World of the Americas. And now we are home once again.

In the course of our journeying we have met the mighty: ancient rulers of proud nations, rulers who thrived on power and hungered for immortality. Their fallen monuments show us the emptiness of their dreams—how their once-great empires became relics in the dust.

> I met a traveler from an antique land
> Who said: Two vast and trunkless legs of stone
> Stand in the desert . . . Near them, on the sand,
> Half sunk, a shattered visage lies, whose frown,
> And wrinkled lip, and sneer of cold command,
> Tell that its sculptor well those passions read
> Which yet survive, stamped on these lifeless things,
> The hand that mocked them, and the heart that fed:
> And on the pedestal these words appear:
> "My name is Ozymandias, king of kings:
> Look on my works, ye Mighty, and despair!"

Nothing beside remains. Round the decay
Of that colossal wreck, boundless and bare
The lone and level sands stretch far away.[77]

From ruined horizons the ghosts of ancient rulers have risen up to meet us. Others too have arisen from the dust, those who long ago were too weak to control their fate. Subjected to the power of others or nature's force, they became the victims of religious ritual or persecution, of conquest or catastrophe. Their names rarely survive, although their deaths can be numbered. Often, painfully often, they are women and children.

Between these extremes of power and powerlessness lies the tender promise of life itself: a blue sky dotted with puffy white clouds, lilies bending in a warming spring breeze, the sensuous swaying of dancers to music, temples of glistening marble, and jewelry of shimmering gold. It is perhaps a world that never fully existed in all its purity, for it was created by ancient imagination and art to transcend the brutality that so often marked life.

In finding this hidden world of beauty, in reconstructing it from the ancient ruins, the archaeologist shows us not only what long-ago dreamers wanted life to be but what life even now could become, if the worst instincts of our civilization did not conspire to prevent it: a world of wisdom and imagination, of creativity and compassion.

And when the ancient mind has created heroes and heroines to embody life's highest risks and ideals, archaeology can show us the world into which they were born, giving us by such discovery new grounds for belief in our own unrealized potential.

For the journey we have taken has been not only an outward one but an inward one as well, exploring the human spirit and its dreams.

Epilogue

Fingerprints in the Dust

IN 1920, WHILE EXPLORING the seemingly empty tomb of an Egyptian official named Meket-rē, archaeologist Herbert E. Winlock uncovered a secret chamber containing wooden models of everyday life on the ancient Nile. The models had been placed there to ensure for Meket-rē an afterlife rich in the same pursuits he had enjoyed when he lived on his great estate and served the pharaoh. Here Winlock describes the moment of discovery:

The beam of light shot in to a little world of four thousand years ago, and I was gazing into the midst of brightly painted little men going this way and that. A tall, slender girl gazed across at me perfectly composed; a gang of little men with sticks in their upraised hands drove spotted oxen; rowers tugged at their oars on a fleet of boats, while one ship seemed floundering right in front of me with its bow balanced precariously in the air. And all of this busy going and coming was in uncanny silence, as though the distance back over the forty centuries I looked across was too great for even an echo to reach my ears. . . .

Four thousand years is an eternity. Just saying it over and over again gives no conception of the ages that have gone by since that funeral [Meket-rē's]. Stop and think of how far off William the Conqueror seems. That takes you only a quarter of the way back. Julius Caesar takes you halfway back. With Saul and David you are three-fourths of the way, but there remains another thousand years to bridge with your imagination. Yet in that dry, still, dark little chamber those boats and statues had stood indifferent to all that went on in the outer world, as ancient in the days of Caesar as Caesar is to us, but so little changed that even the fingerprints of the men who put them there were still fresh upon them. Not only fingerprints, but even flyspecks, cobwebs, and dead spiders remained from the time when these models were stored in some empty room in the noble's house waiting for his day of death and burial. I even suspect that some of his grandchildren had sneaked in and played with them while they were at that house in ancient Thebes.[78]

Like the fresh fingerprints found in Meket-rē's tomb, the humanness of our past sometimes survives as traces in the dust. Such traces, faint as they are, remind us of the common bond of humanity that joins us to those who went before. The thousands of years that seem to separate us from our ancient kin are but illusion, for in the continuum of time we stand as ancient ones too, but to a generation yet unborn.

*   *   *   *

To most, archaeology is viewed as retrospective. And so it is. But archaeology is prospective too, for the skull the archaeologist holds in his hands is as much the symbol of his own future as it is the token of another's past.

That skull, in teaching life's transience, could well lead us to despair, for what hope is there that anything of our lives will endure if that is all that remains? To cynicism too, for if only the skull is left, can it matter if we live selfish or selfless lives?

Such questions were asked three thousand years ago by one who surveyed the ruins of cities already a thousand years dead in his own day. "Mount thou upon the ruined mounds of ancient cities and walk around," he said. "Behold the skulls of earlier and later times. Who is the evildoer? Who is the benefactor?"[79]

These words were written by an anonymous thinker of ancient Babylon. It may surprise us that the people of the past had an ironic sense of history and felt existential pain, but so they did.

The response of some was to construct a theology of the afterlife, to confront the fact of death with the conviction that death as we know it is not the end. But some could not draw comfort from such a philosophy. For them, the problems life posed demanded an answer that rightly could only come from *within* the framework of life as they knew it.

One such thinker called himself *Koheleth,* a word that in Hebrew means "preacher" and is translated in the English Bible as *Ecclesiastes.* Surveying life, Koheleth saw inequity and futility all about him. Yet he sensed a rhythm as well, a balance—realizing that for all of life's destruction there was creation too, that for all of its dissolution there was yet evolving form. "For everything," he said, "there is a season: a time to be born and a time to die, . . . a time to break down and a time to build up, . . . a time to cast away stones and a time to gather stones together."[80]

Like his Babylonian predecessor, Koheleth knew that everything human must ultimately perish. He had seen how "the silver cord is snapped, and the golden bowl is smashed, and the pitcher is shattered at the fountain, and the wheel tumbles into the pit, and the dust returns to the earth as it was."[81]

But his conclusion was not pessimistic, for he came to see that within the very finiteness of life is the opportunity to live fully, that in life's fragileness is the chance to realize the preciousness of being truly alive.

This too is a lesson the murmuring ashes teach: to treasure the mortal moment. For in testifying to the impermanence of human existence they bid us value what can so easily be lost. Archaeology teaches us that we are not alone in this great venture, that others have gone before us—halting or brave—in centuries past, walking through doorways into time . . . and eternity.

Notes

1. Homer, *The Iliad,* trans. Andrew Lang, Walter Leaf, and Ernest Myers (London: Macmillan, 1882), 6:146–149.
2. Horace, *Odes,* 3:30:6.
3. A. Leroi-Gourhan, *Prehistoric Man* (New York: Philosophical Library, 1957), p. 113f.
4. Agatha Christie, *Agatha Christie: An Autobiography* (New York: Dodd, Mead, 1977), p. 364.
5. Sir Leonard Woolley, *Excavations at Ur* (London: Benn, 1954), p. 53.
6. Ibid., p. 71f.
7. Herodotus, *The Persian Wars,* trans. George Rawlinson (London: John Murray, 1862), 2:86–88.
8. For this apt expression see James E. Harris and Kent R. Weeks, *X-Raying the Pharaohs* (New York: Scribner, 1973), p. 21.
9. Herodotus, trans. Rawlinson, 2:90.
10. The translation is my own, based on the version of George A. Barton, *Archaeology and the Bible,* 7th ed. rev. (Philadelphia: American Sunday School Union, 1937), p. 518f.
11. Howard Carter and A. C. Mace, *The Tomb of Tut-Ankh-Amen* (New York: Doran, 1923), p. 141f.
12. From an inscription in the tomb, translated by Hany Assaad and Daniel Kolos, *The Name of the Dead; Hieroglyphic*

Inscriptions of the Treasures of Tutankhamun Translated (Toronto: Benben, 1979), p. 71.

13. Noel Stock, trans., in Ezra Pound and Noel Stock, trans., *Love Poems of Ancient Egypt* (Norfolk, CT: New Directions, 1962), p. 16.

14. Albrecht Goetze, trans., in James B. Pritchard, ed., *Ancient Near Eastern Texts Relating to the Old Testament,* 3rd ed. (Princeton: Princeton University Press, 1969), p. 319.

15. Ibid., p. 395.

16. Sir Mortimer Wheeler, *Civilizations of the Indus Valley and Beyond* (New York: McGraw-Hill, 1966), p. 24.

17. A. L. Basham, *The Wonder That Was India* (New York: Grove Press, 1959), p. 21.

18. Homer, *The Iliad,* trans. Andrew Lang, Walter Leaf, and Ernest Myers (London: Macmillan, 1882), 18:590–606.

19. *Timaeus* 20C–27B, and *Critias* 106A–121C.

20. Heinrich Schliemann, *Troy and Its Remains* (New York: Benjamin Blom, 1968 [1875]), p. 323f.

21. ———, *Mycenae: A Narrative of Researches and Discoveries at Mycenae and Tiryns* (New York: Benjamin Blom, 1967 [1878]), p. 296.

22. Lucian, *Dialogues of the Dead,* 5 ("Menippus and Hermes"); my translation.

23. Prof. Enrico Paribeni of the University of Florence, quoted in A. T. Baker, "Ancient Gifts from the Sea," *Time,* 26 Jan. 1981, p. 69.

24. David L. Shirey, "Italy Celebrates Two Greek Bronzes," *The New York Times,* 10 Oct. 1982, p. H31f.

25. D. H. Lawrence, *Etruscan Places* (New York: Viking, 1966 [1932]), p. 81f.

26. From Pliny's *Letters* 6:20; my translation.

27. From Michele D'Avino, *The Women of Pompeii,* trans. Monica Hope Jones and Luigi Nusco (Naples: Loffredo), p. 127.

28. Josephus, *The Jewish War* 7:8; my translation.

29. Ibid., 7:9.

30. Ezek. 37:4–5, King James trans.

31. Isa. 40:3, King James trans.

32. Quoted in Ronald Harker, *Digging Up the Bible Lands* (New York: Walck, 1972), p. 111f.

33. Edmund Wilson, *The Dead Sea Scrolls, 1947–1969* (New York: Oxford University Press, 1969), p. 98.

34. Revised Standard Version translation.

35. Samuel Pellicori with Mark S. Evans, "The Shroud of Turin Through the Microscope," *Archaeology*, vol. 31, no. 1 (Jan./Feb. 1981), p. 43.

36. Kenneth F. Weaver, "The Mystery of the Shroud," *National Geographic*, vol. 157, no. 6 (June 1980), p. 752.

37. From the preface to Paul Vignon, *Au souffle de l'esprit créateur* (1946), quoted in trans. by Ian Wilson, *The Shroud of Turin* (Garden City, NY: Doubleday, 1978), p. 16. For a possible chemical explanation for the fading of the Shroud image, see Joseph A. Kohlbeck and Eugenia L. Nitowski, "New Evidence May Explain Image on Shroud of Turin," *Biblical Archaeology Review*, Vol. XII, No. 4 (July/Aug. 1986), p. 25.

38. E. R. Goodenough, *The Journal of Biblical Literature*, vol. 81 (1962), p. 141.

39. Sepp Schüller, *Rome*, trans. Lawrence Atkinson (Schwann Travel Guides [Vol. I in the "Christian Italy" Series]; Baltimore: Helicon Press, 1958 [Dusseldorf: Schwann, 1956]), p. 49.

40. See A. Salvagni, *Inscriptiones Christianae Urbis Romae N.S.* (2 vols.; Rome 1922 and 1935), No. 1978, cited by Ludwig Hertling and Eglebert Kirschbaum, *The Roman Catacombs and Their Martyrs* (Milwaukee: Bruce, 1956), p. 157 and 212, n. 14; my translation.

41. George Milligan, ed., *Selections from the Greek Papyri* (Chicago: Ares, 1980), p. xxiv, quoted (with skepticism) from U. Wilcken, *Die griechischen Papyruskunden* (Berlin, 1897) [see Milligan, p. xxiv, n. 2].

42. Edward Gibbon, *The History of the Decline and Fall of the Roman Empire* (London: Strahan and Cadell, 1776–1788), vol. 1, ch. 3.

43. Sir Leonard Woolley, *History Unearthed* (London: Ernest Benn, 1958), p. 41.

44. Leonard Cottrell, *A Guide to Roman Britain* (Philadelphia: Chilton, 1966), p. 268.

45. William Shakespeare, *Hamlet,* Act 5, Scene 1.

46. P. V. Glob, *The Bog People* (Ithaca, NY: Cornell University Press, 1969), p. 31.

47. Tacitus, *Germania,* 12.

48. *Hamlet,* Act 4, Scene 7.

49. Alan Jay Lerner (lyrics), *Camelot; A New Musical* (New York: Random House, 1961), Act 2, Scene 8.

50. Sir Winston Churchill, *The Birth of Britain,* Vol. 1 of *A History of the English-Speaking Peoples* (London: Cassell, 1956), Book 1, Ch. 4, p. 47.

51. Sir Thomas Kendrick quoted in Rupert Bruce-Mitford, *The Sutton Hoo Ship Burial: A Handbook,* 3rd ed. (London: The British Museum, 1979), p. 123.

52. Bruce-Mitford, p. 21.

53. C. W. Phillips, "The Excavation of the Sutton Hoo Ship Burial," *Antiquaries Journal,* April 1940, p. 192.

54. *Beowulf,* vs. 3157–3182.

55. Ibid., vs. 32–52.

56. Bruce-Mitford, dust jacket.

57. Katherine Routledge, *The Mystery of Easter Island* (London: Sifton Praed, 1919), p. 151.

58. John Lloyd Stephens, *Incidents of Travel in Central America, Chiapas and Yucatan* (London: John Murray, 1842), vol. 1, p. 115f.

59. Alberto Ruz Lhuillier, *Archaeology,* vol. 6, no. 1 (Spring 1953), p. 6.

60. ———, *The Illustrated London News,* 29 Aug. 1953.

61. Ibid.

62. Henri Stierlin, *The Pre-Colombian Civilizations* (New York: Sunflower, 1979), p. 14.

63. Jacquetta Hawkes, ed., *The World of the Past* (New York: Knopf, 1963), p. 629.

64. Ruz, *Illustrated London News.*

65. Samuel Taylor Coleridge, "Kubla Khan," vs. 46–54.

66. Alfred M. Tozzer, *Landa's Relación de las Cosas de Yucatan; A Translation* (Cambridge, MA: Peabody Museum, Har-

vard University, 1941; repr. New York: Kraus, 1966), p. 179f.

67. Edward Herbert Thompson, *People of the Serpent* (Boston: Houghton Mifflin, 1932), p. 281f.

68. Ibid., p. 285f.

69. Bernal Díaz del Castillo, *The Discovery and Conquest of Mexico,* trans. A. P. Maudslay (New York: Farrar, Straus, Cudahy, 1956), "Preface," p. xxxiii.

70. Irving A. Leonard, "Introduction to the American Edition," Díaz del Castillo, p. xiiif.

71. John Julius Norwich in Neville Williams, ed., *The Expanding World of Man,* Vol. III of "Milestones of History," (London: Weidenfeld and Nicolson, 1972), p. 104.

72. Díaz de Castillo, 2:4:61, p. 190.

73. ———, 2:5:64–65, pp. 213, 220.

74. ———, 2:4:61, p. 191.

75. Albrecht Dürer, extract from his diary, trans. Mary M. Heaton (adapted).

76. From the *Cantares Mexicanos,* a sixteenth-century anthology of Aztec poetry; adapted from the English translation in Ferdinand Anton, *Ancient Mexican Art* (London: Thames and Hudson, 1969), p. 8.

77. Percy Bysshe Shelley, *Ozymandias.*

78. Herbert E. Winlock, *Models of Daily Life in Ancient Egypt from the Tomb of Meket Rē at Thebes* (Cambridge, MA: Harvard University Press for the Metropolitan Museum of Art, 1955), pp. 3, 7f.

79. Quoted in translation in H. and H. A. Frankfort et al., *The Intellectual Adventure of Ancient Man* (Chicago: University of Chicago Press, 1977 [1946]), p. 217.

80. Eccles. 3:2–5 (passim).

81. Eccles. 12:6–7; my translation.

Suggestions for Further Reading

General

The following works are especially effective general accounts of important archaeological discoveries:

Ceram, C. W. *Gods, Graves, and Scholars,* rev. ed. New York: Knopf, 1967.

Fagan, Brian. *The Adventure of Archaeology.* Washington, DC: The National Geographic Society, 1985.

The following works are anthologies drawn from first-person accounts of archaeologists describing their own discoveries:

Ceram, C. W., ed. *Hands on the Past.* New York: Knopf, 1966.

Deuel, Leol, ed. *The Treasures of Time.* Cleveland: World, 1961.

Hawkes, Jacquetta, ed. *The World of the Past.* New York: Knopf, 1963.

The following works describe the development of archaeology as a science:

Daniel, Glyn. *The Origins and Growth of Archaeology.* New York: Crowell, 1967.

Wheeler, Sir Mortimer. *Archaeology from the Earth.* Baltimore: Penguin, 1956.

Wilson, David. *The New Archaeology.* New York: Knopf, 1975.

The following works describe archaeological theory and method:

Hole, Frank, and Heizer, Robert F., *Prehistoric Archaeology: A Brief Introduction.* New York: Holt, Rinehart, & Winston, 1977.

Macaulay, David. *Motel of the Mysteries.* Boston: Houghton Mifflin, 1979. A spoof satirizing the archaeologist's "conclusions."

Refrew, Colin. *Approaches to Social Archaeology.* Cambridge, MA: Harvard University Press, 1984.

———— and Cooke, Kenneth L., eds., *Transformations: Mathematic Approaches to Culture Change.* New York: Academic Press, 1979.

The following works describe how forgotten languages and scripts have been deciphered:

Chadwick, John. *The Decipherment of Linear B.* Cambridge University Press, 1960.

Cleator, P. E. *Lost Languages.* New York: John Day, 1959.

Friedrich, Johannes. *Extinct Languages.* New York: Philosophical Library, 1957.

Gordon, Cyrus H. *Forgotten Scripts.* New York: Basic Books, 1968.

The following bimonthly periodicals provide well-illustrated and clearly written accounts of recent archaeological discoveries and theories:

Archaeology (Archaeological Institute of America, Box 1901, Kenmore Station, Boston, MA 02215).

Biblical Archaeology Review (Biblical Archaeology Society, 3000 Connecticut Ave., NW, #300, Washington, DC 20008).

Chapter 1: Thunder from the Cave

Bataille, Georges. *Prehistoric Painting: Lascaux or the Birth of Art.* London: Macmillan, 1980.

Breuil, Henri. *Four Hundred Centuries of Cave Art.* Montignac: Centre d'études et de documentation préhistorique, 1952.

Giedion, Sigfried. *The Eternal Present: The Beginnings of Art.* Bollingen Series, XXXV.6.1: New York: Pantheon, 1962.

Leroi-Gourhan, André. *Treasures of Prehistoric Art.* New York: Abrams, 1965.

Pfeiffer, John. *The Creative Explosion.* New York: Harper & Row, 1982.

Radin, Paul. *Primitive Man as Philosopher.* New York: Dover, 1957.

Sieveking, Ann. *The Cave Artists.* London: Thames and Hudson, 1979.

Chapter 2: A Distant Lyre

Chiera, Edward. *They Wrote on Clay.* Chicago: University of Chicago Press, 1959.

Christie, Agatha. *Agatha Christie: An Autobiography.* New York: Dodd, Mead and Company, 1977.

Kramer, Samuel Noah. *History Begins at Sumer.* 3rd ed., rev. Garden City, NY: Doubleday, 1981.

————. *The Sumerians: Their History, Culture, and Character.* Chicago: University of Chicago Press, 1963.

Moorey, P. R. S., ed. *Ur 'of the Chaldees'—A Revised and Updated Edition of Sir Leonard Woolley's Excavations at Ur.* Ithaca, NY: Cornell University Press, 1982.

Chapter 3: Voices from the Tomb

Andrews, Carol. *Egyptian Mummies.* London: British Museum, 1984.

David, Rosalie, ed., *Mysteries of the Mummies.* London: Cassell, 1978.

Hamilton-Paterson, James, and Andrews, Carol. *Mummies.* New York: Penguin, 1978.

Harris, James E., and Weeks, Kent R. *X-Raying the Pharaohs.* New York: Scribner, 1973.

Leca, Ange-Pierre. *The Egyptian Way of Death.* Garden City, NY: Doubleday, 1981.

Romer, John. *Ancient Lives; Daily Life under the Pharaohs.* New York: Holt, Rinehart, & Winston, 1984.

Chapter 4: Behind the Golden Mask

Carter, Howard. *The Tomb of Tutankhamen.* New York: Dutton, 1972.

Desroches-Noblecourt, Christiane. *Tutankhamen.* New York: New York Graphic Society, 1963.

Edwards, I. E. S. *Tutankhamun: His Tomb and Its Treasures.* New York: The Metropolitan Museum of Art and Alfred A. Knopf, 1976.

Erman, Adolf, ed. and trans. *The Ancient Egyptians: A Sourcebook of Their Writings.* Trans. Aylward M. Blackman. New York: Harper & Row, 1966.

Hoving, Thomas. *Tutankhamun: The Untold Story.* New York: Simon & Schuster, 1978.

Pound, Ezra, and Stock, Noel, trans. *Love Poems of Ancient Egypt.* Norfolk, CT: New Directions, 1962.

Chapter 5: Toys in the Dust

Mackay, Ernest. *Early Indus Civilizations.* London: Luzac, 1948.

Possehl, Gregory L., ed. *Ancient Cities of the Indus.* New Delhi: Vikas, 1979.

Wheeler, Sir Mortimer. *Civilizations of the Indus Valley and Beyond.* New York: McGraw-Hill, 1966.

Whitehouse, Ruth. *The First Cities.* New York: Dutton, 1977, Ch. VI, "The Indus Valley."

Chapter 6: The Dark Labyrinth

Cottrell, Leonard. *The Bull of Minos.* New York: Grosset and Dunlap, 1962.

Evans, Sir Arthur. *The Palace of Minos.* New York: Biblo and Tannen, 1964, 4 vols. in 6.

Hood, Sinclair. *The Minoans: The Story of Bronze Age Crete.* London: Thames and Hudson, 1971.

Myres, Joan. *Time and Chance: The Story of Arthur Evans and His Forebears.* London: Longmans, Green & Co., 1943.

Chapter 7: Where Heroes Walked

Blegen, Carl W. *Troy and the Trojans.* New York: Praeger, 1963.

Deuel, Leo, ed. *Memoirs of Heinrich Schliemann.* New York: Harper & Row, 1976.

Poole, Lynn and Gray. *One Passion, Two Loves.* New York: Crowell, 1966.

Schliemann, Heinrich. *Ilios: The City and Country of the Trojans.* New York: Benjamin Blom, 1968 (1881).

———. *Troja.* (1884; New York: Benjamin Blom, 1967 (1884).

———. *Mycenae: A Narrative of Researches and Discoveries at Mycenae and Tiryns.* New York: Blom, 1967 (1875).

Traill, David A. "Schliemann's Discovery of Priam's Treasure: A Reconsideration of the Evidence," *Journal of Hellenic Studies,* vol. 104 (1984), pp. 96–115.

———. "Schliemann's 'Dream of Troy': The Making of a Legend," *The Classical Journal,* vol. 8, no. 1 (Oct.-Nov. 1985), pp. 13–24.

Wood, Michael. *In Search of the Trojan War.* New York: Facts on File, 1986.

Chapter 8: Greek Gods from the Sea

Alsop, Joseph. "Warriors from a Watery Grave," *National Geographic,* vol. 163, no. 6 (June 1983), pp. 820–827.

Bass, George F. *Archaeology Beneath the Sea.* New York: Walker & Co., 1975.

———. *Archaeology Under Water.* London: Thames and Hudson, 1966.

Cleator, P. E. *Underwater Archaeology.* New York: St. Martin's Press, 1973.

Flemming, Nicholas. *Cities in the Sea.* Garden City, NY: Doubleday, 1971.

Lullies, Reinhard, and Hirmer, Max. *Greek Sculpture,* rev. ed., London: Thames and Hudson, 1960.

Muckelroy, Keith, ed. *Archaeology Under Water: An Atlas of the World's Submerged Sites.* New York: McGraw-Hill, 1980.

Schoder, Raymond V. *Masterpieces of Greek Art.* (Chicago: Ares, 1975).

Chapter 9: The Mirrors of Time

Bloch, Raymond. *The Ancient Civilization of the Etruscans.* New York: Cowles, 1969.

Cles-Reden, Sibylle. *The Buried People: A Study of the Etruscan World.* New York: Scribner, 1956.

Dennis, George. *Cities and Cemeteries of Etruria.* 3rd ed., 2 vols.; London: 1878.

Lawrence, D. H. *Etruscan Places.* New York: Viking, 1966.

Moretti, Mario, and Maetzke, Guglielmo. *The Art of the Etruscans.* New York: Abrams, 1970.

Pallotino, Massimo. *Etruscan Painting.* Geneva: Skira, 1962.

Reich, John. *Italy Before Rome.* New York: Phaidon, 1979.

Chapter 10: The Murmuring Ashes

Brion, Marcel. *Pompeii and Herculaneum: The Glory and the Grief.* New York: Crown, 1960.

Gore, Rick. "The Dead Do Tell Tales at Vesuvius," *National Geographic,* vol. 165, no. 5 (May 1984), pp. 556–613.

Grant, Michael. *Cities of Vesuvius: Pompeii and Herculaneum.* London: Weidenfield & Nicholson, 1971.

———— *Eros in Pompeii.* New York: Morrow, 1975.

Pliny the Younger, *Letters,* Book 6, Nos. 16 and 20.

Tanzer, Helen Henrietta. *The Common People of Pompeii: A Study of the Graffiti.* Baltimore: Johns Hopkins Press, 1939.

Chapter 11: Defenders of Israel

Josephus, Flavius. *The Jewish Wars.* Trans. G. A. Williamson; Baltimore: Penguin, 1959.

Yadin, Yigael. *Masada: Herod's Fortress and the Zealots' Last Stand.* New York: Random House, 1966.

Chapter 12: Scriptures in the Wilderness

Allegro, John Marco. *The Treasure of the Copper Scroll*. London: Routledge & Kegan Paul, 1960.

Burrows, Millar. *The Dead Sea Scrolls*. New York: Viking, 1956.

Pfeiffer, Charles F. *The Dead Sea Scrolls and the Bible*. Grand Rapids, Michigan: Baker Book House, 1969.

Vermes, Geza. *The Dead Sea Scrolls in English*. Baltimore: Pelican, 1962.

Wilson, Edmund. *The Dead Sea Scrolls, 1947–1969*. New York: Oxford University Press, 1969.

Chapter 13: Is This a Photograph of Jesus?

Heller, John H. *Report on the Shroud of Turin*. Boston: Houghton-Mifflin, 1983.

Stevenson, Kenneth E., and Habermas, Gary R. *Verdict of the Shroud*. Ann Arbor, Michigan: Servant Books, 1981.

Tribbe, Frank. *Portrait of Jesus?* Briarcliff Manor, NY: Stein and Day, 1983.

Wilson, Ian. *The Shroud of Turin*. Garden City, NY: Doubleday, 1978.

Chapter 14: Echoes from the Catacombs

Bourguet, Pierre de. *Early Christian Art*. Trans. Thomas Burton; New York: Morrow, 1971.

Gough, Michael. *The Origins of Christian Art*. London: Thames and Hudson, 1973.

Mancinelli, Fabrizio. *Catacombs and Basilicas: The Early Christians in Rome*. Florence: Scala/New York: Harper & Row, 1981.

Meeks, Wayne A. *The First Urban Christians: The Social World of the Apostle Paul*. New Haven: Yale University Press, 1983.

Stevenson, J. *The Catacombs Rediscovered: Monuments of Early Christianity*. London: Thames and Hudson, 1978.

Chapter 15: The Faces of Fayum

Hunt, A. S., and Edgar, C. C., trans. *Select Papyri.* 5 vols., repr.; Cambridge, MA: Harvard University Press, 1952.

Lewis, Naphtali. *Life in Egypt Under Roman Rule.* Oxford: Oxford University Press, 1983.

Lindsay, Jack. *Leisure and Pleasure in Roman Egypt.* New York: Barnes and Noble, 1966.

Peck, William H. *Mummy Portraits from Roman Egypt.* Detroit: Detroit Institute of Arts, 1967.

Shore, A. F. *Portrait Painting from Roman Egypt.* London: The British Museum, 1962.

Chapter 16: At Rome's Frontier

Birley, Anthony. *Life in Roman Britain.* New York: Putnam, 1964.

Breeze, David J., and Dobson, Brian. *Hadrian's Wall.* London: Penguin, 1976.

Clayton, Peter A. *A Companion to Roman Britain.* Oxford: Phaidon, 1980.

Scullard, H. H. *Roman Britain: Outpost of the Empire.* London: Thames and Hudson, 1979.

Chapter 17: Bodies in the Bog

Glob, P. V. *The Bog People.* Ithaca, NY: Cornell University Press, 1969.

———. "Lifelike Man Preserved 2,000 Years in Peat," *National Geographic,* vol. 105, no. 3 (March 1954), pp. 219–230.

Chapter 18: The Quest for Camelot

Alcock, Leslie. *Arthur's Britain.* New York: Penguin, 1971.

Ashe, Geoffrey, et al. *The Quest for Arthur's Britain.* London: Pall Mall Press, 1968.

———, *The Discovery of King Arthur.* Garden City, NY: Doubleday, 1985.

Hibbert, Christopher, et al. *The Search for Arthur.* New York: American Heritage, 1977.

Jenkins, Elizabeth. *The Mystery of King Arthur.* New York: Coward, McCann, and Geoghegan, 1975.

Miller, Helen Hill. *The Realms of Arthur.* London: Peter Davies, 1969.

Chapter 19: The Treasure of Sutton Hoo

Bruce-Mitford, Rupert. *The Sutton Hoo Ship Burial: A Handbook.* London: The British Museum, 1979.

Green, Charles. *Sutton Hoo: The Excavation of a Royal Ship-Burial.* London: Merlin Press, 1963.

Grohskopf, Bernice. *The Treasure of Sutton Hoo.* New York: Atheneum, 1970.

Chapter 20: Inside the Great Wall

Cotterell, Arthur. *The First Emperor of China.* New York: Holt, Rinehart, & Winston, 1981.

Hall, Alice J. "A Lady from China's Past," *National Geographic,* vol. 145, no. 5 (May 1974), pp. 660–681.

Li, Yu-ning. *The First Emperor of China.* White Plains, NY: International Arts and Sciences Press, 1975.

Luo, Zewen, et al. *The Great Wall.* New York: McGraw-Hill, 1981.

Qian, Hao, et al. *Out of China's Earth; Archaeological Discoveries in the People's Republic of China.* New York: Abrams, 1981.

Chapter 21: The Fallen Idols

Englert, Father Sebastian. *Island at the Center of the World.* Trans. and ed., William Mulloy; New York: Scribner, 1970.

Heyerdahl, Thor. *Aku-aku.* Baltimore: Penguin, 1960.

———. *The Art of Easter Island.* New York: Doubleday, 1975.

Routledge, Katherine. *The Mystery of Easter Island.* London: Sifton Praed, 1919.

Chapter 22: Temples in the Jungle

Catherwood, Frederick. *Views of Ancient Monuments in Central America, Chiapas, and Yucatan.* London, 1844; repr. Barre, Mass.: Barre Publishers, 1965.

Coe, Michael D. *The Maya.* Rev. ed.; London: Thames and Hudson, 1980.

de Landa, Diego. *Yucatan Before and After the Conquest.* trans. William Gates; New York: Dover, 1977.

Lhuillier, Alberto Ruz. "The Mystery of the Temple of the Inscriptions," in *Archaeology,* vol. 6, no. 1 (Spring 1953), pp. 3–11.

Stephens, John L. *Incidents of Travel in Central America, Chiapas and Yucatan.* London: John Murray, 1842.

Stuart, George E., and Gene S., eds. *The Mysterious Maya.* Washington, DC: National Geographic Society, 1977.

Thompson, J. Eric. *The Rise and Fall of Maya Civilization.* Norman, OK: University of Oklahoma Press, 1984.

Chapter 23: The Well of Sacrifice

Hurtado, Eusebio Dávalos. "Into the Well of Sacrifice, I: Return to the Sacred Cenote," *National Geographic,* vol. 120, no. 4 (October 1961), pp. 540–549.

Littlehales, Bates. "Into the Well of Sacrifice, II: Treasure Hunt in the Deep Past," *National Geographic,* vol. 120, no. 4 (October 1961), pp. 550–561.

Thompson, Edward Herbert. *People of the Serpent.* Boston: Houghton Mifflin, 1932.

Willard, T. A. *City of the Sacred Well.* London: Heineman, n.d.

Chapter 24: Blood on the Sun

Díaz del Castillo, Bernal. *The Discovery and Conquest of Mexico, 1517–1521.* Ed. Genaro García, trans. A. P. Maudslay; New York: Farrar, Straus, and Cudahy, 1956.

Matos Moctezuma, Eduardo. "The Great Temple of Tenochtitlan," *Scientific American,* vol. 251, no. 2 (August 1984), pp. 80–90.

Stuart, Gene S. *The Mighty Aztecs.* Washington, DC: National Geographic Society, 1981.

Vaillant, George C. *Aztecs of Mexico.* New York: Penguin, 1962.

Chapter 25: Child of the Andes

Bingham, Hiram. *Lost City of the Incas.* New York: Duell, Sloan, and Pearce, 1948.

Hemmings, John. *Machu Picchu.* New York: Newsweek, 1981.

Horne, Patrick, and Kawasaki, Silvia Quevedo. "The Prince of El Plomo: A Paleopathological Study," *Bulletin of the New York Academy of Medicine,* Second Series, vol. 60, no. 9 (Nov. 1984), pp. 925–931.

Tierney, Patrick. "Inca Child," *Omni,* vol. 6, no. 11 (August 1984), p. 52ff.

de la Vega, Garcilaso. *The Incas.* Ed. Alain Gheerbrant, trans. Maria Jolas; New York: Avon, 1961.

Von Hagen, Victor. *Realm of the Incas.* (New York: New American Library, 1961.

Chapter 26: Portrait of Pocahontas

Barbour, Philip L. *Pocahontas and her World.* Boston: Houghton Mifflin, 1969.

Cotter, John L., and Hudson, J. Paul. *New Discoveries at Jamestown.* Washington, DC: U.S. Government Printing Office, 1957.

Lankford, John, ed. *Captain John Smith's America.* New York: Harper & Row, 1967.

Riley, Edward M., and Hatch, Charles E., eds. *Jamestown, In the Words of Contemporaries.* Washington, DC: U.S. Government Printing Office, 1955.

Index

About the Author

STEPHEN BERTMAN holds degrees in Near Eastern and Judaic Studies from Brandeis University and in Classics from New York University and Columbia, where he received his doctorate. Dr. Bertman is Professor of Classical and Modern Languages, Literatures, and Civilizations at Canada's University of Windsor in Windsor, Ontario. He is the author of *Art and the Romans* and editor of *The Conflict of Generations in Ancient Greece and Rome.*